THE YOUTH COACH

NATASHA EMIN

FOREWORD BY
BRIAN BELTON

Published by
Bubbles, Hammers And Dreams in 2008
23 Cave Rd
Plaistow
London E13 9DX

First published 2008

ISBN: 978-0-9560092-0-3

Printed and bound in the UK

Dedication

This book is dedicated to 'my mum, my first coach.' I also would like to thank for all their love, support and inspiration over the years: my dad, Prof Stephen Hunt, Philomena Hunt, Vanessa Corby and Jon Handley.

Acknowledgments

Dr Brian Belton, for his unwavering support and belief in me and the book. Fiona Hutchison, for her contribution to this project.

Contents

Foreword **11**
Chapter 1 – Self Harm **15**
What is self harm? 15
Myth Breaking 17
Causes of self harm 19
Why Young People Self Harm 20
The Cycle of Self-Harm 21
Working with a Young Person Who Self Harms –
   The Do's and Don'ts 23
Some useful contacts 24

Chapter 2 - Advocacy **26**
Introduction to Advocacy 26
The Advocacy Process 27
Quick and Easy Overview 29
Peer Advocacy 30
Self advocacy 30
Short Term or Crisis Advocacy 31
Key principles of advocacy 32
Dilemmas faced by advocacy workers 33
When different types of advocacy can be used 34
The Advocacy Charter 35

Chapter 3 – Working with LGB **38**
Working with Young People Who are Gay 38
Why are Some People Gay? 38
Growing Up Gay 39
Coming Out 40
Internalised Oppression 43

Information Sheet for Young People   44
Consequences and Reactions   47
Coming Out Checklist   50
Bi-Sexual Myths   52
The Wrong Label   53
If One of Your Friends Come Out   54
Challenging Homophobia   55
Section 28: Gone but not Forgotten   57
Triangle Badge Coding in WW II Nazi Concentration Camps 59
Lesbian and Gay Quiz   60
Lesbian and Gay Quiz Answers   61

Chapter 4 - Alcohol   **62**
How Much Children and Young People Drink   64
Facts and Figures   65
Strength of Alcoholic Drinks   66
How Alcohol Affects Us   67
Alcohol: The Risks   68
What is Alcoholism?   70
Alcohol and Its Harms   77
Alcohol and the Law   81
Uses and Abuses of Alcohol quiz   82
Alcohol Quiz   83
Alcohol Quiz Answers   83
Alcohol-Related Influences on Young People   84
Example Prompt cards for activity one   85
Strengths Units of Alcohol   86
Alcohol Strengths and Units Score Card   87
Alcohol Law   87
Warning Jokes   88
Play Your Cards Right Question Sheet   89
Play Your Drinks Right Cards   90

Chapter 5 - NLP   **91**
What is NLP? – Neuro-Linguistic Programming   91
Origins of NLP   91
The Physiology of Thinking.   92
Representation System Physiology   93
Logical levels   95
Rapport   98

This is not what I meant at all   100
Getting in a State   102
Reality Leaves a lot to the Imagination   106
The Gatekeepers at the Doors of Perception   112
Language, Trance and Stories   114
Beliefs and Beyond   117

Learning in Action   **121**

Bibliography   **122**

Foreword

This book, unlike many others that may look like it, is not really focused on the problems of young people. In fact it has been written in recognition of the great potential that children and youth have as a constituent part of their humanity.

As a youth and community worker of many years standing, having worked in this field and trained others from Britain, Ireland, Africa, Europe, Asia – from the Falkland Islands to Iceland, from Canada to Hong Kong – I have constantly been impressed and at times overawed by the magnificence, fortitude, bravery, intelligence, and invention of young people. However, over recent years much of my work has been based in the UK and it is a recurring disappointment to see how often professionals and the media portray and treat those broadly defined as 'youth' or 'adolescent' as being inherently problematic; in one way or another, in deficit, that is, lacking in morals and the very nondescript package of 'experience' that the rest of society (the 'adults') have quite perversely and randomly seen to have in abundance.

I have yet to see any evidence that experience makes 'better' people or that the old adage that we 'learn by our mistakes' is a broad truism. In fact it seems what individuals, groups, communities, and societies do repeatedly is to make the same mistakes over and over again. I do not exempt myself from this situation. In fact, because I am very close to those who seek to work with and alongside young people, my impression is that these very groups are more likely to work 'on' their 'clients' as if they were, by the very fact of their youth, pathological; 'in need' of 'help' and 'guidance' and be subjected to 'interventions' by specialist workers. The latter claim greater 'experience', having received 'professional training' focused on 'developing' young people through strategies of 'empowerment' (which assumes a lack of power) to enable (that assumes 'dis-ability') individuals and groups to take a 'full and active' part in society.

I have yet to see anyone 'develop' anyone else or come up with a realistic means of doing this. It seems after years of observation that in the vast majority of cases, our development is reliant on us as individuals to want and find ways of developing ourselves. As an individual, I have always felt that someone looking to develop me is a kind of statement about my current inadequacy (from their perspective). This in turn reminds me of the great blunders of the colonial era (repeating mistakes) wherein particular groups were seen to lack 'religion' and 'civilisation' (and were interestingly, given our society's attitudes to young people, compared to children). I do not know what taking a 'full' part in society would look like or what to be 'active' 'in society' means; ask 10,000 people and they would probably give you 10,000 different answers to the question 'What is it to be active in society?" Some might even say that the most positive reaction to society is not to take part in it at all (as if that were possible).

Work with young people is full of such 'approximate' aims and purposes. Perhaps the most widespread is the ambition to 'educate' them (whether they have asked for it or not). One of the most pompous boasts to be found in youth work is that it 'informally educates' young people. This in effect means that young people are 'educated' without being made fully aware that this is the hidden agenda behind what is overtly labelled as 'fun' or 'leisure activities'. As such, this 'education' is 'covertly' carried out. This is, of course, a contradiction in terms. Covert education is in fact not education at all; it is indoctrination and/or propaganda. There is no agreed agenda, as youth work is funded (directly or indirectly) by the state to achieve 'best practice' (state aims), which in our era is inextricably tied to skill acquisition and employment. The youth service, understood in the broadest sense, is as such dedicated to producing a relatively flexible, relatively skilled, and comparatively cheap (supply to meet demand) work force.

Given the above considerations, I welcome the publication of Natasha Emin's, *The Youth Coach*. In the pages that follow, you will see that Natasha sees young people – who have been hurt as a consequence of some of the worst aspects of our society – as having the means to overcome the experiences that have intruded on their healthy growth as human beings (in many respects a lot of young people have too much experience rather than not enough); that they can find their way to alleviate and/or accommodate pain and hurt by their own efforts. This of course may occur without adults, specialists, or professionals, but as Natasha demonstrates, the benign and 'ready presence' of people that have 'the means to regard' the young first and foremost as people, can work to initiate and speed this process.

The key word in all this, for me, is 'regard'; it involves seeing people as whole beings, whose words and experiences are real and worthy of taking account of. Regard puts 'the other' first, and does not presume deficit. Notions of 'supporting', 'helping', 'enabling' and 'empowering' are not rejected, but they are put aside (they can be called on). But the central focus is that inherent and bright spark that burns within humanity. This is made hot and golden by the warm recognition of our efforts to integrate (build 'integrity' from fragmentation) and dignify (generate dignity in the face of insults to our being) ourselves and others (we cannot have it done without doing it). So rather than 'transplant' my experience, I regard the experience of others; rather than seeking to educate people, I allow people to educate me about them; rather than fool myself that I can give power, I work with others to gain power by the only means that power can be had ... by taking it.

I hope that as you read the pages that follow you will not only see the regard that can be shown to others, but feel that the same regard reaching out to you. If you do, you will return the same and this is the kernel and power of this process; its exponential growth – working with the young is a growth business.

Dr Brian Belton
Senior Lecturer
YMCA Geoge Williams College, London

Release

Some people scream, some people write
Some just get angry, some people fight
Some people can talk, some people can shout
When they have something inside
They've just got to get it out
But if you can't do these things, because you find it too hard
If it feels too unsafe, to let down your guard
If you hide what you feel, because you're scared of rejection
if you think everybody else, expects perfection
If you can't find the words, to express how you feel
Or you feel too ashamed, or it all seems so unreal
It consumes all your being, until it's too much to bear
You have to release it, and hope nobody stares
A silent expression, that no one else sees
So no one can judge you, or laugh at your fears
You know it's not right, and you shouldn't self-harm
But at the time it seems worth it, just to feel calm
I wish I could be normal, and just scream and shout
But until I learn how to
It's my only way out.

Chapter 1 – Self Harm

What is self harm?

The most common form of self-injury is cutting, often of the arms and hands, perhaps of the legs, and less commonly of the face, abdomen, breasts and even genitals. Some burn or scald themselves, others inflict blows on their bodies, or bang themselves against something.

Other ways people injure themselves include scratching, picking, biting, scraping and occasionally inserting sharp objects under the skin or into body orifices. Swallowing sharp objects or harmful substances is well known to doctors. Common forms of self-injury which probably rarely reach medical attention include pulling out one's hair and eye lashes, picking at spots or skin, and scrubbing oneself so hard as to cause abrasion (sometimes using cleaners such as bleach).

Exactly how common or rare self-mutilation is in the general population is difficult to determine because it is such a secretive activity – confidential helplines receive calls from those who have injured themselves for years without telling anyone, due to shame and fear of condemnation. But some studies have found that 11% of students questioned had slashed or cut themselves at some point in their lives.

Self-harm is the intentional cause to harm one's own body by:

Deliberate Self-harm
Self-Injury
Self-Mutilation
Self-Abuse

Self- Wounding
Self-Injurious Behaviour
Self-Mutilative Behaviour
Self-Destructive
Behaviour
Non-Fatal Act
Wrist Cutting
Self-Inflicted Violence

All the previous definitions of self-harm cover the same actions.

Cutting
Burning skin by physical means using heat
Burning skin by chemical means using caustic liquids
Punching hard enough to cause bruises
Head banging
Hair pulling from head, eyelashes, eyebrows and armpits (Trichotillomania)
Poisoning by ingesting small amounts of toxic substances to cause discomfort or damage
Insertion of foreign objects
Excessive nail biting to the point of bleeding and ripping cuticles
Excessive scratching by removing top layer of skin to cause a sore
Bone breaking
Gnawing at flesh
Wound Interference to prevent wounds from healing thus prolonging the affect
Tying ligatures around the neck, arms or legs to restrict the flow of blood
Medication abuse without intention to die
Alcohol abuse (Socially accepted)
Illegal drug use (Socially accepted)
Smoking (Socially accepted)

Cutting and burning are among the most common forms of self-harm. A person who is smoking and drinking is not consciously harming oneself. They are taking part in a socially accepted lifestyle. It is only once these actions become excessive that problems can occur.

There is also a strong correlation between eating disorders and self-harm. This is due to the fact that starvation, binge-eating and self-induced vomiting are forms of self-harm.

Medication abuse in a person suffering with an eating disorder may be in the form of abuse of laxatives and diuretics.

Myth Breaking

For family and friends who have never self-harmed, being faced with this is a daunting task for which they often feel there is no guide. This is why they often make incorrect assumptions.

Self-Harm is a suicide attempt

Self-Harm is not the same as suicide. Somebody who tries to commit suicide feels they have no option and no way out of their pain. However a person who is self-harming is surviving in the best way possible for them at this time. Some people who commit self-harm can become suicidal if they are also depressed, and if they feel self-harm is no longer working for them.

Self-Harm means Borderline Personality Disorder

A borderline personality disorder requires nine criteria, one of which is self-harm. However often doctors can diagnose a person as borderline personality-disordered at first knowledge of self-harm. This is because self-harm itself is not seen as a separate illness so doctors feel the need to categorise it.

Self-Harm means Sexual abuse

Many people who self-harm have experienced some form of sexual abuse. However it does not follow that if someone is self-harming, they must have been sexually abused. Often self-harmers who have had no previous abuse are concerned about the impact of people's assumptions of abuse when self-harm is disclosed.

Mad/Crazy/Schizophrenic/Psychotic people self-harm

Most people who self-harm do not have a serious mental illness. They are struggling with problems such as depression, anxiety and eating disorders which are treatable.

People who self-harm are not mad or crazy; they are in great emotional pain.

She/He has been self-harming for years. They are beyond help.

No person is beyond help. Everyone can live without selfharm if they have access to the right kind of support.

If self-harm does not require stitches or is only superficial, it is not serious

All self-harm is serious. If you discover someone is selfharming, it means they have intense emotional pain and the level/severity of their wounds is irrelevant to this pain. Also the self-harm you may be seeing may only be a small part of the person's current self-harm injuries.

Self-Harm means a danger to others

People who self-harm are highly unlikely to hurt others. This is because they are turning their pain in on themselves, instead of directing it at others.

Self-Harm is attention seeking

Most people who self-harm do not do so for attention. If that was their purpose, there are much easier and less painful ways of achieving this. They are calling out via unspoken communication to ask for love, understanding, support, acceptance and kindness.

Self-Harm is related to Sexual Masochism

A person who self-harms is not the same as someone who has sexual behaviours and fantasies involving the real act of being humiliated, bound or otherwise made to suffer.

Self-Harm is Munchausen's syndrome

Munchausen's syndrome involves a person becoming obsessed about being unwell and will present physical symptoms such as sickness, diarrhoea, fevers etc. A person who self-harms does not have Munchausen's syndrome; the self-harm is caused by real intense emotional pain. The self-harmer often does not go out of their way to seek medical care for the self-harm and often keeps it a secret from many people.

Causes of self harm

So what causes deliberate self-harm? A great deal of factors can contribute to a person self-harming, so let's look first at situations.

Loss of a loved one
Physical abuse such as domestic violence
Sexual abuse such as rape or child abuse
Verbal abuse such as bullying
Childhood neglect from one or both parents
Physical illness or disability
Loss of freedom
Divorce/ relationship problems
Miscarriage
Unwanted pregnancy
Acting as a young carer for an ill / alcoholic parent
Any other trauma

The link between self-harm and a severe trauma is closely linked especially if the person experiencing the trauma has felt unable to ask for or receive help. Any of the above situations can lead up to and create many different kinds of feelings that are often very intense and confusing.

Anger
Anxiety
Bitterness
Fear
Guilt
Grief
Inferiority
Loneliness
Turmoil
Sadness

Self-harm is more complex than an individual reaching for the nearest implement to attack themselves with. These feelings release strong reactions in people's minds that lead to problems within the self.

> Self-hatred
> Self punishment
> Self denial
> Inner turmoil
> Low self-esteem
> A lack of self-control
> Low self-image
> Low self-perseverance
> Low self-respect

Why Young People Self Harm

Mental Release
The release that individuals receive after an act of self-harm is immense. This release can be in the form of many reactions.

> Pleasure
> Pain
> Tension release
> Comfort
> Reassurance of being alive
> Safety
> Satisfaction

Self-harm is not a failed suicide attempt. The majority of people who harm themselves are doing so in order to keep themselves alive. The release they gain enables them to carry on. If this release had not been achieved, they may have moved on to suicidal thoughts. However a person who selfharms is more likely to commit suicide either through a mistake such as too much medication abuse or a misplaced cut. People who self-harm are trying to communicate to you how they feel inside. It is something that they cannot express. The inner turmoil inside them burns bright and they feel unable to put its flames out. This is why people who deliberately self-harm require support and care in order to teach them new ways of thinking and new ways of coping. Every individual requires time, patience, and understanding. Most of these people are not trying to seek attention; they seek something far greater:

> Love
> Trust
> Support
> Kindness
> Acceptance
> Understanding

These are things we all want for ourselves. It is a healthy list of ideals. When a person performs an act of self-harm, they will receive a sense of relief in the form of calm, joy, and well-being due to endorphins being stimulated by the body to help mask the feelings of pain. The result of these endorphins is that self-harm becomes physically and mentally addictive. However the benefit the endorphins bring only lasts for a short period of time, and then the need to self-harm is increasingly overwhelming. This results in a vicious circle of addiction, from which it is very hard to break free. The escape from the cycle can only be achieved if the feelings behind the self-harm are treated as well, otherwise the self-harm will re-occur.

The Cycle of Self-Harm

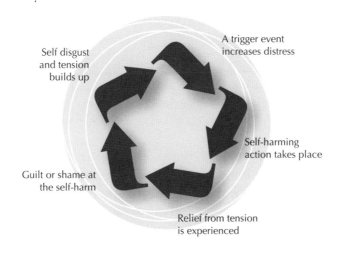

Self disgust and tension builds up

A trigger event increases distress

Self-harming action takes place

Relief from tension is experienced

Guilt or shame at the self-harm

A trigger event may be something which provokes a particular feeling or memory, or which increases the sense of low self-esteem or self-loathing. In working with a young person who wishes to change this behaviour, it is possible to find ways of interrupting the cycle of self-harm. By examining what each stage of the cycle means to them, alternative responses can be identified.

Suggested techniques

There are a number of techniques that might reduce the risk of serious injury, or minimise the harm that can be caused by self-inflicted injury. This list is not exhaustive – different people find different things useful in various situations – so if they do not work at first, try other techniques. Suggested advice includes:

- Stop and try to work out what would have to change in the environment to make you no longer feel like hurting yourself.
- Count down from 10 (9, 8, 7...).
- Point out 5 things, one for each sense, in the present surroundings to bring your attention to the present.
- Breathe slowly, in through the nose, and out through the mouth.
- Try and talk to someone that you trust.
- Recognise that the difficult feelings will pass and that that it is OK to have vulnerabilities.
- Take part in some form of physical activity.
- Treat yourself: try a relaxing bath, aromatherapy, massage, etc.
- Write down your feelings or use art (drawings, paintings, etc.

It is important to make a distinction between self harm and attempted suicide. Of people seen in casualty with deliberate self injury, about a quarter have tried to take their lives, are undecided about living, or have simply left matters to fate.

If the need to cut continues try one of these distractions:

- Using a red water-soluble felt tip pen to mark instead of cut.
- Find a punch bag and vent the anger and frustration.
- Plunging your hands into a bowl of ice cubes - not for too long though.
- Rubbing ice where cutting would otherwise happen.
- Prepare a box of resources including pen, paper, personal stereo with relaxing music, aromatherapy oil (or favourite scent).

What other reasons do people have to harm themselves? A common response is to label the person who self harms as 'attention seeking.' However, a person who self harms may believe this is the only way to communicate how distressed they feel.

Self harm is often a way of dealing with very strong emotions. For some people it gives the relief that crying may bring to others – they might have cried so much that it has ceased to give any relief. Crying is not the only way strong emotions can be expressed. Some self harming people feel so angry and aggressive that they cannot control their emotions – they become afraid that they may hurt someone – and so turn their aggression inwards to get relief.

Working with a Young Person Who Self Harms: The Do's and Don'ts

Do ...
- Listen and take time to hear what the young person says.
- Acknowledge the times when the young person isn't self-harming.
- Understand that young people will self-harm for various reasons and may have different feelings about their self-harm.
- Offer sensitivity and empathy; take time to think about what you want to say.

• Seek out support for yourself, if you feel listened to, you will be better able to support the young person. Be clear with a young person about your limits of confidentiality.
• Offer acceptance and try to let the young person know that you care about what happens to them
• Recognise that self-harm is a coping mechanism which may take some time to be replaced by less harmful alternatives.
• Try to avoid acting out your frustrations with the young person.
• Allow the young person to be in control of the nature and direction of the support you are offering.

Don't...
• Assume the young person is 'out of control.'
• Make the young person promise that they'll stop because you've asked them to. Ignore it and think it'll just go away.
• Be overly critical about what the young person is doing.
• View the young person as a self-harm problem, remember to acknowledge all the other parts of their lives.
• Impose your solutions on the young person. Offer helpful suggestions but don't be offended if these aren't followed through.
• Threaten to withdraw your support if the young person doesn't stop self-harming.
• Expect too much of yourself. You won't and don't need to have all the answers.

Some useful contacts

ChildLine
Freepost 1111
London N1 OBR
Tel: 0800 11 11 (Freephone 24 hours)
Website: www.childline.org.uk

UK's free, 24-hour helpline for children and young people. Trained volunteer counsellors provide comfort, advice and protection. Lines can be busy so please try again if you don't get through the first time.

First Steps to Freedom
7 Avon Court
School Lane
Kenilworth CV8 2GX
Helpline: 01926 851 608 (Every day 10am-10pm)
Tel: 01926 864 473 (information)
E-mail: info@first-steps.org
Website: www.first-steps.org

A confidential helpline for people suffering from general anxiety, panic attacks, obsessive compulsive disorder, anorexia and bulimia. Offers counselling support and information.

National Self-Harm Network
PO Box 7264
Nottingham NG1 6WJ
Website: www.nshn.co.uk

Contact them if you are worried because you self-harm or you are close to someone who does. Provides a free information pack and local links to other organisations.

Self Harm Alliance
Helpline: 01242 578820
(Wednesdays to Sundays 7-8pm)
Website: www.selfharmalliance.org

National survivor led voluntary group supporting any person affected by self-harm, including those who selfharm, their family and friends, and professionals.

Chapter 2 – Advocacy

Introduction to Advocacy

Advocacy is about identifying with, listening to and representing the young person's views and concerns in order that they might bring about beneficial changes that they want in their lives.

At the heart of advocacy is a respect for the dignity of young people and a belief that voicing this respect can have a transforming effect. Advocacy is based on the belief that we all have similar rights, responsibilities and potential for growth. Advocates believe there is a need to challenge the exclusion and discrimination that can be experienced by young people by working with them to understand their legal rights.

Advocacy is about aiming for every young person to have a voice and ensuring they are not ignored and excluded because of difficulties in expressing their views effectively. It is about making things change because their voice is heard and listened to so that young people can make their own choices, take control of their own life and be as independent as they can be, with the support that they require.

Young people are diverse; their needs for support differ and may vary at different times in their lives. Rightly so, a number of forms of advocacy have developed to recognise this diversity. All advocacy types are of equal value and should be looked at as part of an advocacy continuum. What advocacy is used and when, should depend on what is best suited to the individual who seeks advocacy intervention. A variety of advocacy types offers a greater opportunity to recognise the individuality of those that access it.

The important point to make about any type of advocacy

provision is that it should be independent and free from the influence of any organisation that may provide any type of service.

All advocacy types should be based on the principle that an advocate is a means to promoting self advocacy by offering additional skills that may not already be present. Including:

• Some young people do not feel confident or comfortable enough to speak up in public and prefer someone else to do it on their behalf.

Whatever the circumstances, the young person should be in control and at the centre of the advocacy process.

The Advocacy Process

An advocacy initiative can be divided into stages, although in practice these overlap. The time it takes to complete all the stages and the necessary detail will vary greatly, depending on the urgency and complexity of a particular issue, the amount of information needed to be able to act, and the advocacy methods chosen. The basic advocacy cycle is:

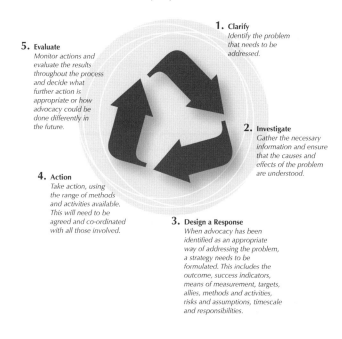

1. Clarify
Identify the problem that needs to be addressed.

5. Evaluate
Monitor actions and evaluate the results throughout the process and decide what further action is appropriate or how advocacy could be done differently in the future.

2. Investigate
Gather the necessary information and ensure that the causes and effects of the problem are understood.

4. Action
Take action, using the range of methods and activities available. This will need to be agreed and co-ordinated with all those involved.

3. Design a Response
When advocacy has been identified as an appropriate way of addressing the problem, a strategy needs to be formulated. This includes the outcome, success indicators, means of measurement, targets, allies, methods and activities, risks and assumptions, timescale and responsibilities.

Outcome	Success Indicators	Means of Measurement	Interim Targets	Allies and Opportunities	Methods and Activities	Risks and Assumptions	Time Scale	Responsibility

Quick and Easy Overview

The questions below provide a quick reference guide for the first three stages of the advocacy cycle. This overview can help you to see the type of information you need and enable you to select the right tools.

What risks are there in getting involved?
What have you done to reduce the risks?
What are the risks if you do not try to address the issue using advocacy work?
What assumptions have you made about the causes and effects of the problem, about those in power, and about your own abilities?

What methods can you use?
Are you confident in using them?
Have they worked before?
Are there alternatives?
Do you have the skills and resources to use them well?

What is the problem?
Is it serious? Is it urgent?

What are the effects of the problem?
How does the problem affect the young person?
Does it have a great effect on certain groups?
If so, who and how?
Do you have enough information?

What are the root causes of the problem?
What is the role of the policies and practices of the organisation?
What is your role?
Is the young person able to participate in decisionmaking?

What do you think needs to be done?
What are your proposals?
What are their advantages and disadvantages?
Are your proposals realistic?
How will you measure success?

Who can bring about change?
Connexions, YOT parents, Youth Services?
Do you have access to them?

Are they open to discussion?
Do they agree they have responsibility for change? Are they able to do something?
Who is addressing the situation?
Can you work with them?
Is their activity effective?
What may need to change?
Are there people who are not yet addressing the issue, but could be persuaded to help you?

Peer Advocacy

The term peer advocacy is used to describe advocacy relationships where both the advocate and the advocacy partner share similar experiences, difficulties or discrimination. This can include looked after children with experience of children's homes, those with mental illness or people with a learning disability living in long stay institutions.

Peer advocacy is often spontaneous in such settings as day centres, residential homes and hospital wards. Often it happens because one person feels more able to speak up than their counterpart and people feel united because of a common cause. The relationship is based on mutual support and empowerment and has the added benefit of a special insight and close rapport being developed between the people involved.

Whilst peer advocacy can be very powerful in challenging services in some circumstances, it can also put the advocate at a disadvantage when they are as disadvantaged as the young person they are trying to support.

Self advocacy

This is speaking up for oneself. It is what most of us do most of the time and is the most satisfactory form of advocacy where it can be achieved. Many young people are good at speaking up for themselves but sometimes find it hard to persuade others to accept or listen to them.

Self advocacy is most commonly recognised in groups that are run and managed by young people. Sometimes the groups may use 'supporters' who are mainly adults, to help with practical issues such as reading and writing and assisting with explanations to aid understanding.

Agendas should be set by the young people and all decisions and choices made by them. They are often groups of young people who use services or have the same interests locally and by working together they can influence and challenge the way services are run.

Groups are a good way for young people to support each other, learn new skills and help to build confidence so that the young people feel more able to speak up for themselves. The self advocacy movement have at times voiced criticism of other forms of advocacy because they feel that other forms promote the view of young people being dependent on others. This however assumes that every young person has the means to advocate for themselves and excludes those who may prefer to have a third person.

Short Term or Crisis Advocacy

This form of advocacy is referred to by many different names including issue based advocacy and casework advocacy. It generally means that any advocacy intervention is to address a specific issue. These can include support to choose a new home, moving out of long stay hospital, child protection cases, parenting issues, personal finances, involvement with the legal system and access to appropriate health and social care. The advocacy input usually ceases as soon as the issue has been addressed and resolved. The strengths of the advocacy model are:

- The relatively fast response times;
- The likely knowledge and skill of the advocate;
- Advocates receive supervision and follow organisational guidelines;
- More people are able to gain advocacy support as advocates work with several young people at the same time;

- This form of advocacy gains more credibility from service providers and their staff because it is seen to be more 'professional'.

The down side to this is the lack of opportunity to offer time to get to know a young person well and support them to recover self esteem and become valued members of their community.

There is also the risk that advocacy may become 'just another service'. If this becomes a good service that has the young person's rights and wishes, at the centre of the process, it could be seen as strength rather than a weakness.

This type of advocacy provision is usually carried out by members of staff from established advocacy projects. Sometimes an advocacy project will have a group of experienced volunteers who are also willing and able to undertake this type of work. The advocate will be supervised and trained to undertake their roles. Key points to this type of short term advocacy are:

- It is temporary and does not involve long term commitment
- It can bring in advocates with specialised knowledge and experience

Advocacy relationships focus on resolving issues and come to an end when targets are met.

Key Principles of Advocacy

Independence
There should be no conflicting interests that limit the action of advocates and advocacy projects. If advocacy is to be effective, it must be independent of any service provider or service commissioner.

Loyalty
The advocate's primary loyalty is to the young person or group they are advocating for. It is an advocate's role to be on the side of the young person they are supporting – not to be impartial – and sometimes they must challenge services or policies if they compromise the young person they represent.

Self-Authority

Advocacy is as much about self-authority as it is about helping to solve short term problems. Young people cannot be empowered by others, but must be supported to take authority themselves. Whenever possible, advocates try to work with the young person to take authority for themselves – realising self-authority

Advocates must treat all young people non-judgementally and respect their concerns and beliefs. It is imperative that advocates should never impose their own views on their clients, even when they disagree with their decisions.

Dilemmas Faced by Advocacy Workers

Independence

A fundamental difficulty for the advocate is the relationship between them and their employers. Frequently the principal employers of advocacy projects have been the Health Service or Local Authorities.

Many young people who need to use advocacy services are often in conflict with either, and the effectiveness of the advocacy provision or partnership can be compromised by the precarious relationship advocacy services often have with their employers.

Loyalty

Advocacy is by its very nature one-sided. An advocate is expected to be loyal to the young person being supported regardless of whether their position is seen as reasonable. Advocates are also expected to be tenacious in supporting and pursuing the position and interests of the young people they support.

Control

New challenges and experiences involve risk. The young person taking control versus protectionism is one of the dilemmas faced by advocacy projects and individual workers, but we have to balance out instinct to protect those who are vulnerable with their right to autonomy.

When Different Types of Advocacy can be Used

- People who need help to make choices and understand what options are available to them will gain the most from immediate short term advocacy.
- People moving from long stay hospitals into the community would need immediate short term advocacy to help them understand their options and make choices about where they would like to live. They may then benefit from being referred to an advocate who can offer long term support and friendship and encourage social inclusion.
- People who are isolated and have little or no known family or friends would benefit from a more long term advocacy.
- People at a day centre or in a residential home can have a say in how services are run and influence future development if they work together as self advocacy groups.
- A self advocacy group that is community based will offer people the opportunity to share their experiences with others, raise awareness of issues that affect people, offer training to others, develop individual confidence, learn about how to deal with issues that affect their lives, and be a source for consultation with partnerships boards and other service provider agencies.
- Peer advocacy has most credibility when others want to understand about the lives of young people, particularly in the present climate of user involvement. Those who provide services are keen to hear what young people have to say. This often causes confusion between self advocacy and peer advocacy.
- Advocacy by a third party, either by a volunteer or a member of staff from an advocacy group, is generally better equipped to address difficult advocacy dilemmas than peer or self advocacy where people involved may be restricted or disadvantaged.

In summary, the various forms of advocacy have points in common. Consideration therefore needs to be given to how best to provide a range of advocacy services so that young people can choose what best suits their individual needs within the limited resources available.

What seems to emerge as the most effective is to have an advocacy organisation, locally based, that provides a range of advocacy services to suit all needs. This would make ease of access to refer to the different specialised sections of the organisation to meet the changing needs of the individuals using the service. For example a dedicated worker to recruit, train and support volunteers to identify advocacy interventions; short term or crisis intervention advocacy workers to manage the advocacy work and a dedicated person to develop and facilitate self advocacy groups.

The Advocacy Charter

The following charter has been produced and adopted by advocacy schemes in London for defining and promoting key advocacy principles.

Independence
The advocacy scheme will be structurally independent from statutory organisations and preferably from all service provider agencies. The advocacy scheme will be as free from conflict of interest as possible both in design and operation, and actively seek to reduce conflicting interests.

Empowerment (see 'control' and 'self-authority' above)
The advocacy scheme will support self-advocacy and empowerment through its work. People who use the scheme should have a say in the level of involvement and style of advocacy support they want. Schemes will ensure that young people who want to can influence and be involved in the running and management of the scheme.

Accountability
The advocacy scheme will have in place systems for the effective monitoring and evaluation of its work. All those who use the scheme will have a named advocate and a means of contacting them.

Supporting advocates
The advocacy scheme will ensure advocates are prepared,

trained and supported in their role and provided with opportunities to develop their skills and experience.

Complaints
The advocacy scheme will have a written policy describing how to make complaints or give feedback about the scheme or about individual advocates. Where necessary, the scheme will enable young people who use its service to access external independent support to make or pursue a complaint.

Clarity of purpose
The advocacy scheme will have clearly stated aims and objectives and be able to demonstrate how it meets the principles contained in this Charter. Advocacy schemes will ensure that young people they advocate for, service providers and funding agencies have information on the scope and limitations of the schemes role.

Putting people first
The advocacy scheme will ensure that the wishes and interests of the young people they advocate for, direct the advocates' work. Advocates should be non-judgemental and respectful of young people's needs, views and experiences. Advocates will ensure that information concerning the young people they advocate for is shared with these individuals.

Equal Opportunities
The advocacy scheme will have a written equal opportunities policy that recognises the need to be proactive in tackling all forms of inequality, discrimination and social exclusion. The scheme will have in place systems for a fair and equitable allocation of advocate's time.

Accessibility
Advocacy will be provided free of charge. The advocacy scheme will aim to ensure that its premises, policies, procedures and publicity promote access for the whole community.

Confidentiality
The advocacy scheme will have a written policy on

confidentiality, stating that information about a young person using the scheme is confidential to the scheme and any circumstances under which confidentiality might be breached.

Chapter 3
Working with LGB
Working with young people who are gay

In parts of this chapter I refer to 'the young girl/lesbian' in the first person. I do this to offer an example of practice, but also to allow the content to be passed on/pointed out to particular young people by workers or parents etc. should this be seen to be helpful/useful by the same.

> '...anti-discriminatory practice – means recognising power
> imbalances and working towards the promotion of change
> to redress the balance of power'
> (Dalrymple & Burke, 2000)

In simple terms, being Gay means that you are sexually attracted to members of the same sex and therefore identify with other Gay people or the larger Gay community. Sexuality is a term used to describe a whole range of feelings, desires, and actions relating to sex.

Why are Some People Gay?

Nobody knows for sure why some of us are Gay and some of us are not. Many theories have been put forward ranging from genetic differences to overbearing parents. The evidence so far suggests that random genetic factors play a part in determining sexuality in the same way they play a part in determining, for example, left-handedness. But it is also accepted that socialisation can have an influence on sexual preferences/choices.

One thing we do know is that no one chooses their sexuality. Some Gay people knew they were different, if not Gay, from as young as five or six. It is said that for most young people, sexuality is determined by the age of 12 or 13 and probably 16 at the latest. By and large, society tends to assume that everyone is, or wants to be, heterosexual. This is known as heterosexism. Some people continue to believe that sexuality is a choice and that we can be persuaded into heterosexuality. By assuming heterosexuality, society gives rise to the dilemma, for young people who know they are gay, whether to hide their sexuality or to come out.

There have been perceptible changes in the way British society views homosexuality, but there is a long way to go before it will accept Gay people in the same way as it does people who are left-handed. This has more to do with society's hang-ups around sex and sexuality than individual Gay people. Often, once people understand that someone who is Gay, their prejudices and fears about homosexuality disappear all together.

Growing Up Gay

For many Gay or bisexual young people, adolescence can be a time of particular anxiety and fear. Many Lesbians and Gays look back on this part of their lives with sadness and regret. There are very few positive gay role models and a lot of hostility towards openly Gay people. Gay teenagers often become painfully aware that they are not like other people and many become withdrawn and lonely, convinced that only they are feeling this way. They learn to hide their true feelings and act as others want them to, for fear of being ostracised, ridiculed, or rejected by loved ones and friends.

Above all, there can be a sense that they are somehow different and abnormal. Some people believe that if they get married, their Gay feelings will disappear. It is unusual for this to happen. Most store up a great deal of stress and anxiety for their later years. Coming out as a Gay parent has particular challenges. Breaking out of a clearly defined role, or even attempting to shift the definition of it, involves tremendous courage and strength. The conflict between their relationship with their spouse and family, and their need to be themselves can be enormous.

Coming Out

Identifying yourself as Lesbian or Gay and disclosing this to other people is often referred to as 'coming out'. There are three main issues associated with coming out:

• 'Coming out' is a necessary and usually positive experience for most young people who grow up Lesbian or Gay. It can take place in the early to mid teenage years. In this period, coming to terms with confusion about identity can affect a young person's social relationships, school work, and self-esteem both negatively and positively.

• Many young Lesbian and Gay people experience critical times when they have to decide who to tell about their sexuality. In making this disclosure, they are often fearful of negative reactions, rejection, and causing upset and distress to the person they are telling. Sometimes a young person may try 'coming out' to a supportive teacher or a school friend as a precursor to talking to parents in order to rehearse their own part and to judge reactions. Receiving a negative reaction can be very distressing.

• Support and reassurances about safety are valuable to people 'coming out'. The availability of secure and confidential groups or contacts can be instrumental in reducing anxiety that is only magnified by feelings of isolation. The presence of role models in the shape of adults who 'come out' and those who offer non-judgmental support and help young people access these groups can be important. Positive treatment by, and contact with, role models can also encourage them to feel confident about their future.

There are several theories about the elements of the 'coming out' process. Each has its own emphasis but all of them are developmental models, which regard 'coming out' as a series of stages. These stages do not necessarily last the same length of time and there is no one age when the whole process begins and ends. These stages can be described as follows:

Sensitisation

In this stage a person generally begins to feel 'different' to other people of the same sex. Sometimes they recognise that they are not very interested in people of the opposite sex, but more often they feel they are not really interested in things which are supposed to be appropriate for their sex. Most people report just feeling unusual when they compare themselves to other people of their sex. Commonly this happens before or in early adolescence when friendships and relationships between the sexes begin to change.

Confusion about identity

There are usually four elements which contribute to confusion about identity:

- Feeling that perceptions of the self are altering
- Feeling and experiencing heterosexual and homosexual sexual arousal
- Sensing the stigma surrounding homosexuality
- Lacking knowledge about homosexuality

Some young people who think they are Lesbian or Gay will try to deny it to themselves and even seek help to eradicate their feelings. Others will try and avoid thoughts and feelings which remind them that they have homosexual inclinations. In these situations young people can avoid getting any information about sexuality in order to avoid confirming their suspicions about their orientation.

Some young people have great difficulty in managing their relationships with peers and family. They may avoid situations in which they may encounter opportunities for heterosexual pairing so that they are not forced to deal with their lack of sexual interest in members of the opposite sex or have it exposed. They may, alternatively, persevere with heterosexual relationships to try and 'convert' themselves and/or conceal their homosexuality from others. In some extreme cases young people may try to avoid confronting their feelings by expressing strong homophobia or turning to drink and drugs in order to find temporary relief from them.

Finally, some young people fall back on a strategy of redefining their feelings and behaviour in such a way as to convince themselves that it is not really homosexual. For example, they may describe their experiences as a 'phase' or a 'one-off', or they may put them down to extreme emotional or physical circumstances such as the break-up of a relationship or drunkenness at a party. In this stage, feelings are becoming more concrete. Young people may well have partners of both sexes and may well find their moods and feelings shifting as they feel more or less certain about their identity. This period often lasts throughout adolescence.

Assuming a Lesbian or Gay identity

Clearly, living with confusion about identity is emotionally exhausting and potentially destructive. For some people, this period is followed quite quickly by a stage in which they come to accept their Lesbian or Gay identity and are able to express it in a positive way. For both young men and women, growing up mixing with other young Gay people – in social settings or through support groups – can help them feel able to accept who they are. For some people, particularly in larger towns and cities, Lesbian and Gay support groups provide a safe environment for 'coming out'. Elsewhere local and national Lesbian and Gay telephone helplines provide a listening ear for people who want support.

Commitment

The final stage in the process of 'coming out' involves becoming being Lesbian or Gay openly and recognising that it is a central aspect of, 'who I am', and, 'how I want to live my life'. People begin to feel that homosexuality is a valid way of life and develop a sense of contentment with being lesbian or gay. They often have the experience of falling in love at this time and, perhaps as a result, feel more confident, fulfilled, and able to combat the social stigma that they may suffer.

At this time some Lesbian and Gay people begin to feel proud of their sexuality. The expression of this pride in being Lesbian or Gay is a powerful force in challenging the stigma attached to homosexuality by people with prejudiced attitudes and provides positive role models to others less sure about 'coming out'.

Internalised Oppression

When 'difference' is valued negatively, prejudice results. Prejudice results from the inequalities, judgements, and misuses of power that infiltrate everyday life.

Oppression means the systematic mistreatment of a certain group sometimes because of the misinformation and poorly informed conclusions about them. Internalised oppression is when an oppressed group takes on the negative messages and acts them out self destructively, resulting in damage to their health, safety, well being, creativity and potential.

DIFFERENCE SEEN AS THREAT TO STATUS QUO
Implicit or explicit conclusions are made about a certain group: 'not good enough', 'abnormal, strange, weird' 'bad, wrong, dangerous'.

MISINFORMATION AS "TRUTH"
These conclusions and misconceptions then become the common, accepted, "truth" about this group. This results in pressure on the group to change or adapt their behaviour.

The pervasive assumptions and conclusions introduce self-doubt in the oppressed group: 'Maybe there is something wrong with us'; 'no one will like us unless we change'; 'it's true, some of us are like that.

Compensating for the prejudice and mistreatment becomes a way of life for the oppressed group. Personal development creativity is second to maintaining good relations with the oppressors.

PREJUDICE AS A REAL THREAT TO SAFETY AND SECURITY
Rationalising: that's the way it is what can you do?
Appeasing: anything for a quiet life
Ghettoising: keep to your own kind
Justifying: we're not that bad
Siding with theoppressors: don't spoil it for the rest of us don't let the side down
Compromising, accepting limitations: don't argue back ignore them
Defending: don't give them more ammunition

The oppressed undermine themselves to end the conflict

The constant pressure to change (usually parts of the person's identity which cannot be changed – gender, race, sexuality etc.) creates a huge, internal conflict inside the person. If unresolved, this conflict results in the oppressed taking on the work of the oppressors by undermining themselves. They begin to believe the negative messages. The oppressors 'truth' becomes their truth. Life is an apology. They turn the anger and injustice in on themselves, resulting in self-destructive behaviour and thoughts. They become addicted to compromising in order to be accepted, sacrificing individuality and identity.

The burden of new information increases the risk of damage

The self-destruction and undermining within the oppressed group either goes unnoticed or gets misinterpreted as further 'proof' of the groups 'inferiority.' This further extends the misinformation about the group and increases the pressure on the oppressed group to change.

Information Sheet for Young People

Coming Out

There are several stages in the process of coming out. From a young Gay personal perspective:

Coming Out to Yourself

Acknowledging that you are Gay can take many years. Some of us probably hoped these feelings were 'just a phase', and sometimes they might be. But people often realise that these feelings are not just a phase and feel they have to find a way of accepting them and deal with the fact that they are sexually attracted to members of our own sex.

This realisation is the first stage of coming out. There is no hard and fast rule when this point is reached. For some it happens in their teens, for others it may happen much later in life.

Some people describe this time of accepting their sexuality as though they were riding an emotional rollercoaster. One day they felt happy and confident and ready to tell everyone; the next day they felt confused, scared and relieved that they hadn't. In this case they may want to talk to someone who understands what this is like.

So You Still Want to Come Out?

This is a nerve racking time – the fear of rejection is likely to be immense. Bear in mind that there are many ways to tell someone that you are Gay.

It may be helpful to ask yourself some of the questions that come up later in this guide, as it is more than likely that others will ask you them at some point. Don't rehearse your answers but think of your reasons – it will make you and your discussions stronger and more assured.

Many Gay people describe how important it is to first tell someone outside the family. Make sure it's someone you trust and who you believe to be open-minded and supportive. Be careful if you decide to confide in a teacher at school – they may be obliged to tell someone else what you have told them. Find out the school policy on confidentiality before you go ahead.

If you have decided to tell your family, it may be easier to talk to one parent before the other. You could then ask them for help to approach the other. Sometimes brothers and sisters are a good starting point as they maybe likely to understand more about homosexuality or bisexuality. Make sure you understand why you are opening up to them. One of the best reasons to come out to your family is to become closer to them.

There are a number of typical responses that parents, particularly, are known to say such as, 'How can you be sure?'; 'I went through a phase like this at your age'; 'You'll grow out of it'; 'You haven't tried hard enough with the opposite sex', and 'How can you know at your age?'

We have listed them here because they may help you to think of your answers to them. You might find it helpful to discuss these questions first with a trusted friend or a Lesbian and Gay helpline or switchboard.

Support for Your Family

This can be a traumatic time for some members of your family. You may feel unable to answer all their questions or to deal with all of the issues that come up for them. They, in turn, may not feel comfortable talking about homosexuality or bisexuality with you. There are several organisations that offer support to parents who are coming to terms with their son's or daughter's sexuality.

This can be a difficult time if your happiness is dependent to some degree on your family's reaction. If this is the case for you, we would advise that you talk it over with someone who has been through it already – perhaps your local gay switchboard or helpline.

How Should I Tell Them?

There is no rule that says you have to sit down and talk to others about this; there are other ways.

You might like to write to them first and give them time to react in their own way. This is probably a better approach if, for example, you live a long way from your family or friends. Remember that you have probably taken a long time to get used to the idea yourself and others might need the same amount of time. Writing a letter allows you to take your time and to compose your thoughts carefully and clearly. It can also give the person you are writing to space to react and consider the news before discussing it with you. This could be a useful approach if you are expecting a very hostile or negative reaction.

If you decide to talk face to face, remember not to rush it or to do it when one of you is in a hurry or distracted. It probably won't help to memorise a script either – you can guarantee that some people do not respond in a predictable manner. If you are worried about their reaction, tell them of your fears, and that you don't want to hurt them but need to be honest with them. Remember to listen to what they have to say – it should be along the lines of a chat, not a speech or lecture!

When Should I Tell Them?

When it comes to coming out, timing is an important consideration. Choose the moment carefully – do it when you (and they) have lots of time - not last thing at night when you are likely to be more tired and emotional.

Think about the way you are feeling, allowing for nerves, which are perfectly natural under the circumstances. Don't do it if you are feeling angry or emotionally sensitive – this will affect what you say and how you say it. For obvious reasons don't do it when you are drunk (even if you think you need a drink to steady your nerves).

And remember – only when you are good and ready. A friend once said that he knew he was ready to tell his family only when he realised that, if he had to, he could live without their support. Fortunately for him (and his family), this didn't happen.

Consequences and Reactions

So you've told someone. You are either balancing on the edge of an erupting volcano or dancing with joy on the moon (or both!). Some people describe a huge weight being lifted from their shoulders, of feeling euphoric and giggly and childlike again.

> **'My parents refused to talk about it. They dismissed it and said they didn't want the subject brought up again. I decided that I was going to continue to live my life as a Gay man. I stopped going home as often as I used to and attending family occasions. It is only now, three years later, that they have begun to broach the subject with me.'**

Don't feel guilty about it – go on and enjoy yourself. You deserve it! The thrill of revealing something long kept hidden can give a tremendous sense of relief.

Use this new-found energy wisely and remember that close friends and family may be worried that you have changed out of all recognition. Reassure them that you have changed – and for the better and that you are simply exploring a new, more complete you.

Most people will experience many positive reactions. For example, 'We're so pleased you could tell us' or 'Well we had already guessed and were just waiting for you to say something'. Some Gay people have also been met with the response, 'So am I'.

> **'My family say that they accept that I am Gay but they don't want to see me being affectionate with another man. They say that they won't be able to cope with it.'**

If it hasn't gone too well - don't lose heart. Time is a great healer and things will get better. If you are experiencing rejection from some close friends, ask yourself if they were really so close that they couldn't support you through this. If your family is reacting badly, this is in all probability, normal. They may be experiencing a whole range of emotions including shock, feelings of grief, guilt, blame, disappointment, and lots of pain.

> **'I was at a wedding recently and everyone was there with their partners. I was upset that I couldn't bring mine. Everyone asked the usual embarrassing questions about girlfriends and I just had to smile and make excuses. I didn't want to row with my family about it, but it's just not fair.'**

Remember how long it took for you to come to terms with being Gay. Many parents will feel a loss in some way – perhaps of future grandchildren, weddings, and other family gatherings. This can blur their happiness and their love for you. At the end of the day, your parents are still your parents and, in time, few reject their children because they are Gay. If they go quiet on you, give them time to react and the opportunity to think about what you have told them. If they ask lots of questions, it's a good sign. It may help to think of it as though it is in your interests to respond to them – they are likely to be the same ones that you have asked yourself many times along the way.

> **'My dad said, 'You're still my son and I'm proud of you.' He'd been very homophobic up to then.'**

If things are so bad that you feel like giving up with the whole process of coming out, it's important to talk to someone about your fears and concerns. Again your local switchboard, helpline or Gay Men's Health Project can offer you support and guidance.

Coming Out at Work

There are some circumstances where coming out could seriously affect your job security and promotion prospects because of informal or institutional discrimination.

Telling Your Doctor

It is worth mentioning, too, that if you disclose your sexuality to your general practitioner (doctor), they may record these details in your medical records. These medical records can be accessed by a range of organisations for many different purposes.

There comes a time to stop talking and to get on with living your (new) life exactly how you want to. It's time to meet other Gay and bisexual people and to explore your sexuality safely and confidently.

A common reaction to this statement, especially in rural areas is: 'Fine – but where do I start?' Remember that being Gay is about expressing yourself in the way YOU want to. Despite the stereotypes, there is no single way of being Gay. We are all as different as any other group of people.

Going out with friends and meeting new ones at clubs or parties can be great. But the 'scene' isn't for everybody, and it's not everything there is to being Gay. Most towns and cities have gay social groups and Gay men's health projects. These can be excellent places to meet new people and to find out what there is to do locally and most will arrange to meet first time visitors beforehand.

As with any group of people, there will be some you get on with and some you won't. If you feel that you have little in common with the gay people you have met so far, you could try different ways of contacting more gay people, for example as pen pals, or through the many special interest Gay groups (like Gay men's choirs or Gay football supporters networks) – look them up in Gay Times.

Coming Out Checklist

Telling people that you're Gay is a deeply personal thing. Some people choose to be very open about their sexuality, while others are more discreet. Whatever the case, if you're considering coming out, then you have to be prepared to handle the impact it will have on your life. Here are some of the things to think about first.

Why Now?
There is no set time as to how long you should wait. Gay men and women who have come out will each have different experiences, but most will have been fairly confident about their sexuality first. So ask yourself if this is something you've been thinking about for a long time, or a sudden urge that you haven't had a chance to think through, because basically once you're out, it's very difficult to get back in.

Who Shall I Tell?
Kick off by confiding in someone you trust who can give you the support and understanding you need to tell others. Also use the opportunity to talk through the way you feel with them. If this is first time you've ever discussed your sexuality, it might help you get a clearer perspective on things.

What Shall I Say?
There is no script, but if you can come out with honesty and openness, and you show respect for the person you're telling, then at the very least you can expect a similar response. Just be aware that you don't have to justify your sexuality to anyone but yourself.

What if They React Badly?

Sadly, this is something you should always be prepared for. Whether its shock or anti-Gay sentiment that has prompted a negative response, try to stay calm. Stress that being gay doesn't make you any different as an individual, and that essentially you're still the same person as you were before you came out. All that's changed is their perception of you, so don't despair if at first they don't respond as you had hoped. Attitudes can often be changed, and you may find they just need some time to get their head around things. If you are worried about violence or being thrown out of your home, make sure in advance that a friend can put you up.

What Will Coming Out Mean to Me?

It can mean as much or as little as you want. What's important is that you're comfortable with your sexuality, and confident that coming out is the right step for you to take.

Exploring Your Sexuality

Straight, Gay or bi, you don't have to label yourself immediately, or ever. However, exploring your feelings and accepting your sexuality is important. So where do you start?

Get a Grip

The most important thing is to be honest with your feelings and see where they take you. Sexuality is no easy ride; you have a whole host of emotions to get a grip of, not to mention the physical side of things.

Virtually everyone will have feelings for someone of the same sex at some stage in their life. This does not mean they have to rush out and buy a rainbow sticker for their car. It is just a natural part of sexual development. However if these feelings are more frequent or long lasting then it may be more significant.

Labels and Stereotypes

Don't rush into giving yourself a label and coming out in public. This is a very personal thing and you probably want to be comfortable with your feelings before broadcasting to the world.

Unfortunately some people can't accept any other sexual orientation to their own as being normal. They are mistaken in their thinking, and you must remember that you are not doing anything wrong or immoral. However such prejudice can, understandably, be hard to take and you may be tempted to keep your sexuality quiet. While this may seem fine in the short term, do you really want to hide this side of you forever? Be true to yourself; you have every right to be comfortable with who you are.

Play Safe

Just because you have decided your sexual orientation does not mean you have to get jiggy with the first person you fancy. Give it time, and only get passionate when you feel ready. Don't forget that it doesn't matter if you are Gay, straight or bi. Have safe sex to reduce the risk of pregnancy and getting any sexually transmitted diseases. It's also a good idea to know the law.

Find Out More

You don't have to change yourself or your social life just because you have a different sexual preference to the rest of your mates. Life can tick on as normal; however it may help you to read books or articles written by or about people who have gone through the same thing as you.

You may also want to join a club or society run by Gay people for Gay people, it will give you support of people who understand exactly what you are going through, and will be especially helpful if you feel uncomfortable discussing everything with your mates. Although it is worth remembering that you won't necessarily like every Gay person you meet, just like you don't like every straight person you meet.

Bi-Sexual Myths

For confidential advice and support call the Lesbian and Gay Switchboard on 020 78377324.

More and more people are openly choosing to identify themselves as bisexual – yet many of us don't really know what this sexual preference actually means. Bisexuals have to like both men and women equally. Wrong – there is no right or wrong way to be bisexual. You are the person who determines your sexuality. If you only date girls but are also attracted to guys, you can be bisexual. The same goes for people who date guys, but still like girls.

Some people believe that your sexuality is always changing. If you are bisexual, you could be attracted to men and women at different points in your life. It is the individual that you find attractive, not their gender.

Bisexuals are promiscuous; they can't hold down a committed monogamous relationship.

Wrong. News flash: a bisexual can fall in love and hold down a relationship. Being bisexual might mean you feel attracted to guys and girls, but it doesn't give you license to be unfaithful to your partner, or to expect him/her to accept another person into your love life. Relationships still have the same rules.

Bisexual people are just playing around; they can choose to be straight.

Wrong. You don't choose your sexual orientation, you just feel it, be you straight, Gay or bi. There's a difference between being straight and falling in love with a person of the opposite sex and being bi and doing so. In the latter case, this doesn't mean that they aren't attracted to people of the same sex still or that they aren't bisexual. It doesn't mean you have turned straight.

Bisexual people are just denying that they are Gay.

Wrong. Being bisexual is different to being Lesbian or Gay. However, because your sexuality can change over time, it is possible to be bisexual for a while and then to be Gay or straight. But most consider themselves bisexual for their whole lives, and they tend not to change the category from one relationship to the next.

The Wrong Label

Having doubts about whether it's basic curiosity or something more permanent? If you've labelled yourself as Gay or straight, this doesn't mean the label can't change. You came out young and were completely OK with it, but now you have feelings for someone of the opposite sex.

What does this mean?

If you believe your attraction to this person goes beyond the boundaries of your sexuality, why not take the opportunity to ask yourself what these boundaries actually mean, and how they came to be imposed.

Gay or straight, it's just a category. A means of labelling yourself to conform to the way our society defines sex, gender, and relationships. The trouble is our feelings and desires don't always sit so easily in this way, which can lead to a great deal of grief and confusion. Forget about the labels for a moment.

You're attracted to an individual, and the important thing is that you feel able to come to terms with these emotions. Try to have a heart to heart with the person in question. This will go some way to finding a positive outcome to this situation, not just in terms of your feelings for him/her, but the bigger picture, too.

You've always considered yourself straight but you've recently been having feelings for people of the same sex. Are you Gay?

Your attraction to other guys/girls can mean a lot or a little. What's important is that you find a comfortable way to make sense of these feelings.

The fact is everyone comes to terms with their sexuality in different ways. Some people are sure they're Gay from a very early age, while others go through periods of uncertainty or confuse same sex admiration for sexual attraction. So don't fret about labelling yourself just yet. Ultimately, all that matters is that you're true to yourself.

If One of Your Friends Come Out ...

Out of the blue, your best mate tells you they're Gay/bi/a Lesbian. How do you deal with it and how can you be there for them?

Firstly, coming out is a big step for anyone. You should be flattered that your mate chose to confide in you. It shows that they hold you in high regard. Don't freak out at the prospect though; it is unlikely they want to jump into bed with you. Instead think about the following:

• First impressions: When you meet new people, do you ask if they have a boyfriend OR girlfriend? By not assuming other people's sexual orientation, you let your friends know that it's OK to tell you if they're Gay.

• Stereotypes: Don't expect your friend to change their appearance and their identity because they're not straight. They haven't become a different person overnight. They won't suddenly acquire dress sense and aspirations of a career in hairdressing, nor will they rush to shave their head and join the pool team. Sexual identity is part of your personality; it doesn't and shouldn't shape your whole life.

• Deal with it: You might not share the same beliefs as your mate, but you can still support them. Chances are that they were scared to tell you, especially if they thought you wouldn't approve of their decision. It's completely normal to feel uncomfortable and nervous, especially if you haven't known Gay people before. Try to remember that nothing has changed about your friend except that they have been more honest with you.

• Lean on me: You don't have to be Gay in order to support Gay rights; it is simply a striving for equality. If you want to help make a difference, get out there and do something; however do consider your mate. They may not have told anyone but you, so don't go parading them about as a Gay icon/ needy cause. Don't turn their emotional rollercoaster into gossip; they have enough to deal with.

• Talk on: Don't clam up after the initial conversation you and your mate have about them coming out. If you keep talking about it, you will both be better able to be comfortable with the situation.

Challenging Homophobia

Assertive Confrontation
This model of challenging behaviour has been taken from assertiveness training and can be useful for challenging oppressive remarks or behaviour.

It is not about 'winning', and doesn't attempt to change the other person's views, but asks the person to change their behaviour so your working environment is safer for everyone.

Guidelines

1 Start with a statement of your own opinions (eg: I feel offended, irritated, annoyed, put down, confused, challenged)

2 Describe the behaviour specifically (eg: by that joke, that word, that assumption, that comment)

3 Field the other person's statements and repeat your own (eg: Your friends may find the joke funny, but I find it offensive. I have got a sense of humour, and I find that joke offensive I am not picking on you. I'd tell anyone who made that comment ...)

4 Ask for a specific change (eg: We do not allow any forms of prejudice in this youth club and ask you not make comments, jokes, or discriminate like that again when you are using this club.)

5 If the person then asks if you are Lesbian, Gay, or bisexual you can say that your objection and/or request has nothing to do with your sexual orientation but is about their behaviour

6 You can specify the negative consequences if they do not agree to change their behaviour. Ensure that these are realistic.

7 Move things on as quickly and smoothly as possible.

Things to Consider

- Be aware of your organization;s equal opportunities policy.
- Ensure that the whole team uses the same approach to tackling homophobia.
- Not all young people are heterosexual and even though they may not be out in your service, any homophobic comments will have an effect on them.
- Homophobic language is a form of bullying and putting people down; if you have a strong antibullying attitude this could be used to challenge people's behaviour.
- When something is described as 'Gay' (e.g. a pair of trainers, haircut, or a pool cue) it can be used to challenge the inappropriate

language being used – ask the person what they mean by the use of the word 'Gay'.

• You will, on some occasions, be asked to declare your sexual orientation – as with all other private personal information your sexual orientation has nothing to do with those you work with. It can be challenging and unnerving to deal with such a delicate issue, but it can also be used as an opportunity to get your service users to look at their own attitudes towards diversity, prejudice, and discrimination.

Section 28: Gone but not Forgotten

From midnight on Monday 17th November 2003, a piece of legislation described as 'pernicious' and 'homophobic' was repealed. The removal of the 15 year old statute was welcomed by Gay commentators and human rights activists alike who believed it made Gay people second class citizens under a 'deeply offensive law.'

Section 28 of the Local government Act 1988 prohibited local authorities from 'promoting' homosexuality or Gay 'pretend family relationships', and prevented councils spending money on educational materials and projects perceived to promote gay lifestyle.

The section's removal from British law has been described as a 'triumph for 21st century tolerance over 19th century prejudice.'

When it was introduced, Section 28 galvanised the Gay rights movement leading to protest rallies and campaign groups such as OutRage! and Stonewall. The actor Sir Ian McKellen says he 'came out' in disgust at the legislation. In the Lords, the debate about the ruling was interrupted by three Lesbians who abseiled into the chamber from the public gallery. Perhaps more memorably, the day before the section became law, four campaigners invaded BBC studios while Sue Lawley was reading the news.

Ben Summerskill, the Director of Stonewall, said 'Its removal is hugely important because it is totemic ... It was deliberately designed to stigmatise and demean 3 million people.' Sue Saunders, of the group Schools Out, which supports Lesbian and Gay teachers, said she was delighted: 'What we are dealing with is ignorance, fear, and embarrassment.'

Section 28 was first proposed in a private member's bill by the independent peer Lord Halsbury, and tabled in December 1986. It was not aimed at 'responsible homosexuals,' he said, adding that there were homosexuals who 'would no more molest little boys than a responsible adult would molest little girls.' However, there were 'sick' homosexuals, 'suffering' symptoms of promiscuity, exhibitionism, 'boasting' of homosexual achievements, and an urge to persuade other people that their way of life was a good one. Lord Halsbury said they acted as 'reservoirs' for venereal disease.

One of the main focuses of Tory outrage was a children's book called *Jenny Lives With Eric and Martin*, which showed a little girl in bed with her father and his boyfriend.

While no one was ever prosecuted under the section, it had a wide effect, with libraries refusing to stock Gay newspapers, Gay websites blocked on school and college computers, and Glyndebourne Touring Opera being forced to abandon a staging of *Death in Venice*. Section 28 did not directly legislate for schools, but it prompted staff self-censorship. Teachers were confused about what they could say and do, and were unsure whether they could act when pupils faced homophobic bullying.

A recent Stonewall survey of 300 secondary schools found that 82% of teachers were aware of verbal incidents linked to homophobia and 26 knew of physical attacks. Only 6% of schools had anti bullying policies designed to combat homophobia.

The mental health charity MIND says two in three Gay and Lesbian people are likely to have mental health problems. Many believe this is due to homophobia that has been fuelled by Section 28.

However one agency in North London continued to run young Gay men's, young Lesbian and older Lesbian groups throughout the duration of Section 28. It was funded by the ILEA. The worker in charge was able to do this as he claimed he was working with young people to explore their sexuality and was 'promoting' nothing. There is nearly always a way through!

Triangle Badge Coding in World War II Nazi Concentration Camps

The shape was chosen by analogy with the common triangular road hazard signs in Germany that denote warnings to motorists. Here, a triangle is called inverted because its base is up while one of its angles points down. In addition to colour coding, some groups had to put letter insignia on their triangles to denote country of origin: red triangle with a letter: 'B' (Belgians), 'F' (French), 'I' (Italians), 'P' (Poles), 'S' (Republican Spanish), 'T' Czechs), 'U' (Hungarians). The most common forms of the badge were:

Black inverted triangle
• A vagrant
• A Roma or Sinti (Gypsy)
• A woman jailed for 'anti-social behaviour' i.e. a Lesbian, a prostitute or woman who used birth control.

Green inverted triangle
• a regular criminal.

Pink inverted triangle
• a homosexual.
Purple inverted triangle
• a Jehovah's Witness and Bible Students.

Red inverted triangle
• a political prisoner. The colour red was probably chosen because it represented the Communists, bitter political enemies that the Nazis hated most (and the first to be officially outlawed).

Two superimposed yellow triangles forming the Star of David
• a Jew, including Jews by practice or descent.

Pink inverted triangle superimposed upon a yellow one, making the Star of David
• a homosexual Jew.
Yellow inverted triangle superimposed over a black triangle, or 'voided' black inverted triangle superimposed over a yellow triangle

Lesbian and Gay Quiz

1. Can you name 5 famous Lesbians?
2. Can you name 5 famous Gay men?
3. What is Polari?
   a) An old slang language used by Lesbians and Gay men   to hide their identity
   b) The name of the first fully licensed Gay club in London
   c) A support group for older Lesbians and Gay men
4. Young gay and bisexual men are more likely to practise unsafe sex? T F
5. 1 in 5 young lesbian and gay teenagers have attempted suicide? T F
6. Can you name the popular symbol of Lesbian pride that originated in the Nazi concentration camps?
7. Can you name the popular symbol of Gay pride that originated in the Nazi concentration camps?
8. Who was the first professional athlete to come out whilst actively competing?
9. The rainbow flag representing Lesbian, Gay and Bisexual communities has six colours; can you name them?
10. What is the age of consent for Lesbians and Gay men?
11. Currently what percentage of British schools have fully inclusive anti-bullying policies which address homophobic bullying?
12.Currently what percentage of secondary school teachers say they are aware of verbal homophobic bullying?

Lesbian and Gay Quiz Answers

1. KD Lang (singer), Ellen DeGeneres (comedian, Actress), Martina Navratilova (Tennis Player), Pam St. Clement (Pat Evans in Eastenders), Sam Fox (Page Three Model), Sandy Tokgsvig (comedian, actress), Julie Goodyear (Bet Lynch on Coronation Street), Tracy Chapman (singer)

2. George Michael (Singer), Rupert Everett (Actor), Dale Winton (Presenter), Steven Gately (singer), Simon Callow (Actor), James Dean (Actor), Jean- Paul Gaultier (Designer), Sir John Gielgud (Actor)

3. a) An old slang language used by Lesbians and Gay men to hide their identity

4. True

5. True

6. Black inverted triangle

7. Pink Inverted Triangle

8. Martina Navratilova

9. Red, Orange, Yellow, Green, Blue, Indigo

10. 16

11. Between 5-6%

12. 80%

Chapter 4 – Alcohol

Slang
Booze, juice, sauce, grog.

Background
Alcohol is produced by fermenting fruits, vegetables or grains. It is found in drinks like beer, lager, wine, alcopops, cider, and spirits such as whiskey or gin. Alcoholic drinks range in strength and are measured as a percentage (%) per volume; the higher the percentage, the stronger its effect.

The Effects
• Over 90% of the adult population enjoy a drink. For most people, alcohol has a relaxing effect and helps them feel more sociable.
• Alcohol can become a problem for some if they drink as a way of blotting out difficult or troubling issues in their lives.
• In increasing quantities, alcohol affects people in different ways. Sometimes, speech can become slurred, co-ordination affected and emotions heightened.
• The intensity of the effects depends on the strength of the alcoholic drink, plus the rate and amount consumed.
• Other factors that influence the effects of alcohol include the weight of the drinker, their mood and surroundings, and how recently they ate.
• Hangovers make the drinker feel ill for a period of time, usually hours, but sometimes even for days.

The Risks
• Alcohol is a depressant drug. If you're feeling down, it will make you feel worse.

• A regular, long-term drinking habit can lead to physical as well as psychological dependency.

• Tolerance can develop, which means that over time, you'll need to drink more to get the same effect.

• A long term, heavy drinking habit may cause serious damage to internal organs. It can also cause skin problems, trembling (the shakes), obesity, brain damage, mood swings, and personality changes.

• Getting very drunk can lead to loss of consciousness. Users then have a slight risk of choking to death on their own vomit.

• Drinking too much can lead to alcohol poisoning. This can kill, although it is fairly rare.

The Law

It is illegal to sell alcohol to anyone under 18 (unless they're 16-17 and eating a meal in a restaurant). The legal limit for driving in the UK is 80mg of alcohol per 100ml of blood. The number of drinks it takes to reach this level varies from person to person. Safety experts advise not to drink at all if you are going to drive.

If you are planning on drinking

Men who drink more than half to two pints of lager/beer, or three glasses of wine a day run the risk of serious health problems.

• Women should not exceed a pint or a couple of glasses of wine per day.

• Mixing alcohol with other drugs is seriously dangerous. This is because drink serves to slow down the nervous system (controlling heart and breathing rate). Combined with other depressant drugs, the body could shut down altogether.

Advice and support

In the UK, more than 2 million families are affected by someone with a drinking problem. Alateen provide support for young people living with a problem drinker in the family. Call 020 7403 0888

Young people and alcohol
Some of the main reasons young people start to drink are:

- Curiosity and experimentation
- To appear mature
- To conform with expectations of what young people do.

By 14 or 15 young people say they drink to:

- Have fun and experience the buzz
- Get drunk and experience losing control
- Socialise with others – alcohol can break down boundaries
- Enhance sex appeal. (Hughes, 1997)

Young people are more tolerant of drunkenness than adults. They consciously plan to binge-drink and think their friends approve of this. (Wright, 1999).

How Much Children and Young Peoiple Drink

Most young people drink.
Over 80% of 11-16 year-olds have tried alcohol. For a quarter of those surveyed, this means having 'a few sips'.

Young people are drinking more.
Among young people who drink, the amount consumed has doubled since 1990 to ten units a week. The mean consumption among 15 year-old boys who drink is nearly 12 units a week and nine units for girls.

Young people are drinking more regularly.
The proportion of 11-15 year-olds who drink alcohol at least once a week rose from 20% in 1988 to 24% in 2000.

Greater numbers are binge drinking and regularly getting drunk.
15 and 16 year-olds in the UK are more likely to get drunk or binge-drink than most of their European counterparts.

Drinking starts when children are in primary school.

Just under 5% of eight-year-olds have consumed a whole alcoholic drink. 14% of girls and 21% of boys aged 10 and 11 drink each week. By the age of 13, drinkers outnumber those who don't drink. Over half of 14 and 15 year olds drink each week.

Regular use of alcohol is starting younger.

The age children start to drink unsupervised – as part of their own social lives – is more significant than their first taste of alcohol. Drinking tends to start at home in the presence of parents.

Facts and Figures

- Alcohol-related illnesses and injuries cost the National Health Service up to £3bn a year on hospital services.
- It costs British industry more than £2bn a year due to alcohol-related absenteeism and poor work performance.
- Alcohol misuse can have a devastating effect on families, and is strongly linked to partner and child abuse as well as neglect.
- About a quarter of young people drank in the last week.
- Children and young people make a very fast transition between drinking very little under adult supervision, to drinking independently as adults by the time they are about 16. In recent years, the amount they drink has doubled.
- Almost a third of 15-16 year-olds binge drink (drink more than five units in one session) and get drunk at least three times a month. This is higher than most other European countries.
- Children and young people are particularly vulnerable when they drink. Small amounts of alcohol can get them drunk and impair their judgement so they take risks. The recommended daily benchmarks for alcohol consumption are based on adults drinking. No recommendations exist for children and young people. We do not yet know the long-term consequences of their drinking.

Strength of Alcoholic Drinks

All alcoholic drinks contain pure alcohol (ethanol) in varying amounts. One way of comparing the amount of alcohol in different types of drink is by using 'units'. Each of the following contains one unit:

- A small glass of wine (9% ABV) = 1 UNIT (note: many wines are 11 or 12% ABV)
- A 25ml pub measure of spirit (40% ABV) = 1 UNIT
- A half pint of ordinary strength lager/beer/cider (3.5% ABV) equals 1UNIT
- It takes about an hour for the adult body to get rid of one unit of alcohol. This may be slower in young people.

Recommended daily benchmarks for drinking
- Men who regularly drink four or more units and women who regularly drink three or more units are putting their health at risk.
- Binge drinking' is when on one occasion, men drink more than eight units and women drink more than six.
- No guidelines exist for children or young people's drinking.
- For the under 18s, 'binge-drinking' often means drinking to intoxication.

The sensible drinking benchmarks for adults are:
- Three to four units a day for men
- Two to three units a day for women

How much adults drink
When asked what alcohol they drank in the previous week:
- Nearly two thirds of men and half of women drank alcohol at least once
- 17% of men and 11% of women drank on five or more days
- 20% of men and 8% of women had been binge drinking on at least one day.

Men have traditionally drunk more than women but there are concerns that women are drinking more and a greater proportion at hazardous levels. Women drink the most between the ages of 16 and 24.

Drink	Quantity	Units
wine	125ml glass (11-12% ABV)	1.5
	175ml glass (11-12% ABV)	2
	75cl bottle (9-10% ABV)	6.8 - 7.5
	75cl bottle (11-12% ABV)	8 - 9
	50ml sherry, port, madeira, vermouth, martini	1
Lager	330ml bottle (4-5% ABV)	1.5
Beer	440ml can (4-5% ABV)	2
Cider	440ml can (8-9% ABV)	3.5 - 4
	500ml can (1 pint), (4-5% ABV)	2 - 2.5
	500ml can (8-9% ABV)	4 - 4.5
	440ml can low alcohol beer (1.2% ABV)	0.5
Spirits	25ml pub measure (40% ABV)	1
Alcopops	300ml bottle of 'alcopop' (4-6% ABV)	1.3 - 2
	20cl bottle of 'alcopop' (13.5% ABV)	2.7

How Alcohol Affects Us

After alcohol has been drunk, it passes through the stomach and small intestine and is absorbed into the bloodstream. From there it travels to the rest of the body, including the brain. It is processed out of the body by the liver.

Alcohol is a 'depressant'. This means it slows down the reactions in your brain. It lowers some of your inhibitions, making you feel reckless. Alcohol affects your physical coordination, reaction times, and judgement.

It takes the liver one hour to process one unit of alcohol. No matter how fast we drink, the liver can only work at this pace.

The effects of alcohol can be felt between ten and 20 minutes after drinking, and sooner on an empty stomach. The effects vary depending on:

- How much you drink and how quickly
- What you drink (fizzy drinks and stronger drinks such as spirits, are absorbed more quickly)
- How used you are to drinking
- Your size and weight
- Your gender – Women are more affected by alcohol than men as they tend to be smaller and have more relative body fat and less water in their body. As a result the concentration of alcohol is higher.

Children and young people will be more affected by alcohol than adults who are generally bigger and have developed more tolerance to alcohol. The same amount of alcohol will make them feel more drunk, and could cause damage, alcohol poisoning, and coma much sooner than it would in adults.

Alcohol: The Risks

Alcohol is linked to:
- Liver damage – fatty liver, alcoholic hepatitis, and cirrhosis.
- Cancer – of the mouth, larynx, pharynx, and oesophagus, liver, stomach, colon and rectum, and possibly breast.
- Heart disease and high blood pressure – Alcohol raises the blood pressure. However, for those who are prone to heart disease (men over 40 and post-menopausal women) a small amount of alcohol can help protect against heart disease;
- Problems with the digestive system such as inflammation of the stomach lining, irritating ulcers, damage to the pancreas.
- Psychiatric disorders – heavy drinking is closely linked with mental health problems, including clinical depression (HEA 1997) and with an estimated 65% of suicides. Up to one third of young suicides have drunk alcohol at the time of death. The rise in teenage male suicide rates has been attributed to a rise in alcohol consumption.

- Reproductive problems – In men, temporary impotence and longer-term loss of potency, shrinking testes and penis and reduced sperm count. In women the menstrual cycle can be disrupted, it may increase the risk of miscarriage, can result in low birth weight babies, birth defects and foetal alcohol syndrome.
- Alcohol dependence – 7% of adults in the UK are mildly dependent on alcohol and 0.1% are moderately to severely dependent. It can happen to anyone.

Deaths due to alcohol
- 6400 died as a direct result of alcohol in 1998.
- Alcohol contributes to an estimated 30,000 deaths each year including accidents, suicides, and a whole range of diseases.

Mixing alcohol with other drugs
Alcohol reacts with some medicines and can be dangerous when used with illicit or recreational drugs:
- Alcohol + other depressant drugs = risk of coma
- Alcohol + amphetamines = further reduces ability to make judgements, especially about keeping safe
- Alcohol + Ecstasy = even more dehydration and extra pressure on the liver and kidneys
- About 15% of 14-15 year-olds have taken drugs and alcohol together

Children and young people affected by others' drinking
- Roughly 920,000 children live in a home where one or both parents are problem drinkers.
- These children will not necessarily be in need or at risk, but alcohol misuse has been linked to neglect and emotional, physical abuse, and sexual abuse.

Alcohol can interfere with the way families function
- Parents can become undependable, inconsistent, and unpredictable.
- Children often take on the role of carer for parents or other children.
- Daily routines, family rituals and social lives are disrupted.
- Children can find it hard to make or keep friends or invite them home.

There is some debate about whether children with problem-drinking parents are more likely to have their own problems with alcohol than children who have not. Recent views suggest this may not be the case.

Children have different strategies for coping with a problem-drinking parent or carer for example, withdrawing, blaming themselves, developing behavioural difficulties or creating a supportive network outside the family. Some actively attempt to order and structure their lives despite problems.

Alcohol and ethnic and religious diversity

White pupils are the most likely of all ethnic groups in the UK to drink alcohol. 19% of white 15-16 year-olds drink at least once a week compared to 8% of black pupils and 3% of Asians. However, drinking among the Asian population has recently risen, particularly among the Hindu community.

The use of alcohol is prohibited or disapproved of in Hinduism, Sikhism, Islam, Buddhism and many Christian denominations for example, the Salvation Army, and Quaker Society. In reality, some members of these faiths do use alcohol.

What is Alcoholism?

Alcoholism, also known as alcohol dependence, is a disease that includes the following four symptoms:
• Craving: A strong need, or urge, to drink
• Loss of control: Not being able to stop drinking once drinking has begun
• Physical dependence: Withdrawal symptoms, such as nausea, sweating, shakiness, and anxiety after stopping drinking
• Tolerance: The need to drink greater amounts of alcohol to get 'high.'

For clinical and research purposes, formal diagnostic criteria for alcoholism also have been developed. Such criteria are included in the Diagnostic and Statistical Manual of Mental Disorders (4th Edition) published by the American Psychiatric Association, as well as in the International Classification Diseases, published by the World Health Organisation.

Is alcoholism a disease?

Yes, alcoholism is a disease. The craving that an alcoholic feels for alcohol can be as strong as the need for food or water. An alcoholic will continue to drink despite serious family, health, or legal problems.

Like many other diseases, alcoholism is chronic, meaning that it lasts a person's lifetime. It usually follows a predictable course, and it has symptoms. The risk for developing alcoholism is influenced both by a person's genes and by his or her lifestyle.

Is alcoholism inherited?

Research shows that the risk for developing alcoholism does indeed run in families. The genes a person inherits partially explain this pattern, but lifestyle is also a factor. Currently, researchers are working to discover the actual genes that put people at risk for alcoholism. Your friends, the amount of stress in your life, and how readily available alcohol is also are factors that may increase your risk for alcoholism.

But remember: risk is not destiny. Just because alcoholism tends to run in families doesn't mean that a child of an alcoholic parent will automatically become an alcoholic too. Some people develop alcoholism even though no one in their family has a drinking problem. It is also the case that not all children of alcoholic families get into trouble with alcohol. Knowing you are at risk is important, because then you can take steps to protect yourself from developing problems with alcohol.

Can alcoholism be cured?

No, alcoholism cannot be cured at this time. Even if an alcoholic hasn't been drinking for a long time, he or she can still suffer a relapse. To guard against a relapse, an alcoholic must continue to avoid all alcoholic beverages.

Can alcoholism be treated?

Yes, alcoholism can be treated. Alcoholism treatment programmes use both counselling and medications to help a person stop drinking. Most alcoholics need help to recover from their disease. With support and treatment, many people are able to stop drinking and rebuild their lives.

Which medications treat alcoholism?

A range of medications is used to treat alcoholism. Benzodiazepines (Valium® Librium®) are sometimes used during the first days after a person stops drinking to help him or her safely withdraw from alcohol. These medications are not used beyond the first few days, however, because they may be highly addictive. Other medications help people remain sober. One medication used for this purpose is naltrexone (ReVia™). When combined with counselling, naltrexone can reduce the craving for alcohol and help prevent a person from returning or relapsing to heavy drinking. Another medication, disulfiram (Antabuse®), discourages drinking by making the person feel sick if he or she drinks alcohol.

Though several medications help treat alcoholism, there is no 'magic bullet.' In other words, no single medication is available that works in every case and/or in every person. Developing new and more effective medications to treat alcoholism remains a high priority for medical research.

Does alcoholism treatment work?

Alcoholism treatment works for many people. But just like any chronic disease, there are varying levels of success when it comes to treatment. Some people stop drinking and remain sober. Others have long periods of sobriety with bouts of relapse. And still others cannot stop drinking for any length of time. With treatment, one thing is clear, however; the longer a person abstains from alcohol, the more likely he or she will be able to stay sober.

Do you have to be an alcoholic to experience problems?

No. Alcoholism is only one type of an alcohol problem. Alcohol abuse can be just as harmful. A person can abuse alcohol without actually being an alcoholic – that is, he or she may drink too much and too often but still not be dependent on alcohol. Some of the problems linked to alcohol abuse include not being able to meet work, school, or family responsibilities; drunk-driving arrests and car crashes; and drinking-related medical conditions. Under some circumstances, even social or moderate drinking is dangerous, for example, when driving, during pregnancy, or when taking certain medications.

How can you tell if someone has a problem?

Answering the following four questions can help you find out if you or a loved one has a drinking problem:

• Have you ever felt you should cut down on your drinking?
• Have people annoyed you by criticising your drinking?
• Have you ever felt bad or guilty about your drinking?
• Have you ever had a drink first thing in the morning to steady your nerves or to get rid of a hangover?

One 'yes' answer suggests a possible alcohol problem. More than one 'yes' answer means it is highly likely that a problem exists. If you think that you or someone you know might have an alcohol problem, it is important to see a doctor or other health care provider right away. They can help you determine if a drinking problem exists and plan the best course of action.

Can a problem drinker simply cut down?

It depends. If that person has been diagnosed as an alcoholic, the answer is 'no.' Alcoholics who try to cut down on drinking rarely succeed. Cutting out alcohol, that is, abstaining, is usually the best course for recovery.People who are not alcohol dependent but who have experienced alcohol-related problems may be able to limit the amount they drink. If they can't stay within those limits, they need to stop drinking altogether.

If an alcoholic is unwilling to get help, what can you do about it?

This can be a challenge. An alcoholic can't be forced to get help except under certain circumstances, such as a violent incident that results in court-ordered treatment or medical emergency. But you don't have to wait for someone to 'hit rock bottom' to act. Many alcoholism treatment specialists suggest the following steps to help an alcoholic get treatment:

• Stop all 'cover ups'. Family members often make excuses to others or try to protect the alcoholic from the results of his or her drinking. It is important to stop covering for the alcoholic so that he or she experiences the full consequences of drinking.

• Time your intervention. The best time to talk to the drinker is shortly after an alcohol-related problem has occurred – like a serious family argument or an accident. Choose a time when he or she is sober, both of you are fairly calm, and you have a chance to talk in private.

• Be specific. Tell the family member that you are worried about his or her drinking. Use examples of the ways in which the drinking has caused problems, including the most recent incident.

State the results
Explain to the drinker what you will do if he or she doesn't go for help--not to punish the drinker, but to protect yourself from his or her problems. What you say may range from refusing to go with the person to any social activity where alcohol will be served, to moving out of the house. Do not make any threats you are not prepared to carry out.

Get help
Gather information in advance about treatment options in your community. If the person is willing to get help, call immediately for an appointment with a treatment counsellor. Offer to go with the family member on the first visit to a treatment program and/or an Alcoholics Anonymous meeting.

Call on a friend
If the family member still refuses to get help, ask a friend to talk with him or her using the steps just described. A friend who is a recovering alcoholic may be particularly persuasive, but any person who is caring and non-judgemental may help. The intervention of more than one person, more than one time, is often necessary to coax an alcoholic to seek help.

Find strength in numbers
With the help of a health care professional, some families join with other relatives and friends to confront an alcoholic as a group. This approach should only be tried under the guidance of a health care professional who is experienced with this kind of group intervention. Get support: It is important to remember that you are not alone. Support groups offered in most communities

include Al-Anon, which holds regular meetings for spouses and other significant adults in an alcoholic's life, and Alateen, which is geared to children of alcoholics. These groups help family members understand that they are not responsible for an alcoholic's drinking and that they need to take steps to alcoholic family member chooses to get help.

Certain people should not drink at all

- Women who are pregnant or trying to become pregnant
- People who plan to drive or engage in other activities that require alertness and skill (such as using highspeed machinery)
- People taking certain over-the-counter or prescription medications
- People with medical conditions that can be made worse by drinking
- Recovering alcoholics

Does alcohol affect older people differently?

Alcohol effects do vary with age. Slower reaction times, problems with hearing and seeing, and a lower tolerance to alcohol's effects put older people at higher risk for falls, car crashes, and other types of injuries that may result from drinking.

Older people also tend to take more medicines than younger people. Mixing alcohol with over-the-counter or prescription medications can be very dangerous, even fatal. More than 150 medications interact harmfully with alcohol. In addition, alcohol can make many of the medical conditions common in older people, including high blood pressure and ulcers, more serious. Physical changes associated with aging can make older people feel 'high' even after drinking only small amounts of alcohol. So even if there is no medical reason to avoid alcohol, older men and women should limit themselves to one drink per day.

Does alcohol affect women differently?

Yes, alcohol affects women differently than men. Women become more impaired than men do after drinking the same amount of alcohol, even when differences in body weight are taken into account. This is because women's bodies have less water than men's bodies. Because alcohol mixes with body water, a given amount of alcohol becomes more highly concentrated in a woman's body than in a man's. In other words, it would be like dropping the same amount of alcohol into a much smaller pail of water. That is why the recommended drinking limit for women is lower than for men. In addition, chronic alcohol abuse takes a heavier physical toll on women than on men. Alcohol dependence and related medical problems, such as brain, heart, and liver damage, progress more rapidly in women than in men.

Is alcohol good for your heart?

Men who have two or less drinks per day and women who have one or less drinks per day are less likely to die from one form of heart disease than are people who do not drink any alcohol or who drink more. It's believed that these smaller amounts of alcohol help protect against heart disease by changing the blood's chemistry, thus reducing the risk of blood clots in the heart's arteries.

If you are a non drinker, however, you should not start drinking solely to benefit your heart. You can guard against heart disease by exercising and eating foods that are low in fat. And if you are pregnant, planning to become pregnant, have been diagnosed as alcoholic, or have another medical condition that could make alcohol use harmful, you should not drink.

If you can safely drink alcohol and you choose to drink, do so in moderation. Heavy drinking can actually increase the risk of heart failure, stroke, and high blood pressure, as well as cause many other medical problems, such as liver cirrhosis.

When taking medications, must you stop drinking?

Possibly. More than 150 medications interact harmfully with alcohol. These interactions may result in increased risk of illness, injury, and even death. Alcohol's effects are heightened by medicines that depress the central nervous system, such as sleeping pills, antihistamines, antidepressants, anti-anxiety drugs, and some painkillers. In addition, medicines for certain disorders, including diabetes, high blood pressure, and heart disease, can have harmful interactions with alcohol. If you are taking any over-the-counter or prescription medications, ask your doctor or pharmacist if you can safely drink alcohol.

Alcohol and Its Harms

Alcohol plays an important and useful role both in the economy and in British society generally. The Strategy Unit calculated that the cost of alcohol-related harms in England is up to £20bn per annum. These harms include:

- harms to health
- crime and anti-social behaviour
- loss of productivity in the workplace
- social harms, such as family breakdown

The Costs of Alcohol Related Harm

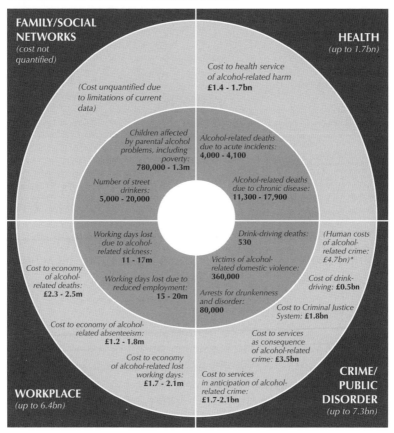

FAMILY/SOCIAL NETWORKS
(cost not quantified)

(Cost unquantified due to limitations of current data)

Children affected by parental alcohol problems, including poverty:
780,000 - 1.3m

Number of street drinkers:
5,000 - 20,000

HEALTH
(up to 1.7bn)

Cost to health service of alcohol-related harm
£1.4 - 1.7bn

Alcohol-related deaths due to acute incidents:
4,000 - 4,100

Alcohol-related deaths due to chronic disease:
11,300 - 17,900

Working days lost due to alcohol-related sickness:
11 - 17m

Cost to economy of alcohol-related deaths:
£2.3 - 2.5m

Working days lost due to reduced employment:
15 - 20m

Cost to economy of alcohol-related absenteeism:
£1.2 - 1.8m

Cost to economy of alcohol-related lost working days:
£1.7 - 2.1m

Drink-driving deaths:
530

Victims of alcohol-related domestic violence:
360,000

Arrests for drunkenness and disorder:
80,000

(Human costs of alcohol-related crime:
£4.7bn)*

Cost of drink-driving: **£0.5bn**

Cost to Criminal Justice System: **£1.8bn**

Cost to services as consequence of alcohol-related crime: **£3.5bn**

Cost to services in anticipation of alcohol-related crime:
£1.7-2.1bn

WORKPLACE
(up to 6.4bn)

CRIME/ PUBLIC DISORDER
(up to 7.3bn)

Nos. affected/No. of incidents

Cost of harm

How the Population Drinks

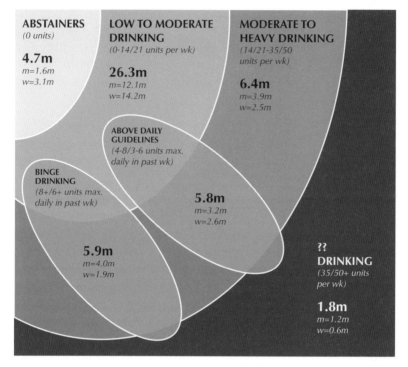

Alcohol Harm Strategy

Young people under the age of 16 are drinking twice as much today as they did ten years ago, and report getting drunk earlier than their European peers. As part of a longterm alcohol harm reduction strategy, it is vital that young people are educated to make responsible choices about their drinking behaviour.

Education and Young People

• Young people need clear and accessible information in order to make responsible choices about drinking behaviour.
• Issues are specific health effects to alcohol-related crime, school exclusion and unsafe sex.
• Young people themselves should be consulted on what is most likely to make a difference.

Multi-component approach

• It will be equally important to address the lack of evidence relating to the effectiveness of interventions for children and young people outside the classroom.

• In non-traditional settings such as youth centres and leisure facilities. As part of this, young people themselves should be consulted on what is most likely to make a difference.

Tolerance

• Refers to the way the body gets used to the repeated presence of a drug, which means that higher doses are needed to maintain the same effect.

• The body learns to tolerate the drug in the system. Alcohol, barbiturates, heroin and amphetamine are all drugs to which the body can build up tolerance.

Dependence

• (Dependency, dependent) describes a compulsion to continue taking a drug in order to feel good or to avoid feeling bad. When this is done to avoid physical discomfort or withdrawal, it is known as physical dependence.

• When it has a psychological aspect (the need for stimulation or pleasure, or to escape reality) then it is known as psychological dependence.

• Physical dependence is when someone has taken drugs in quantity for a time and comes to rely on the use of a drug in order to feel well and for their body to function 'normally'.

• It mainly happens with depressant drugs like alcohol, barbiturates, heroin, or tranquillisers. However, the deep depressions and even suicidal feelings can follow cocaine and ecstasy use.

Young Peoples Drinking

Young people drink for a variety of reasons including a rite of passage, to say that they have tried alcohol, to have fun and to get drunk, and to show their maturity and experience.

Although young people may at times drink in an uncontrolled way, most will not go on to develop serious problems. Common problems young people experience are the effects of severe intoxication and accidents. Studies suggest that young people combine alcohol and sex, especially prior to their first sexual experience and that there is a link between drinking before sexual activity and unsafe sex.

There is also an association between alcohol and crime. A recent report showed that 25% of young prisoners had been drinking when they committed their crime.

Risk factors – young people
- Youth offending
- School exclusion
- In or having been looked after by a Local Authority
- Children with a history of problems/abuse
- Sexual exploitation
- Children having learning difficulties
- Children from families with a history of substance misuse

Social implications of excessive drinking
- Family
- Problems at work
- Financial difficulties
- Homelessness and vagrancy
- Crime including violent and sexual crime
- Drink driving
- Victimisation
- Impact on education and training

Brief Interventions
- Feedback
- Responsibility
- Advice
- Menu
- Empathy
- Self-Efficacy

Authorities recommend that men should drink no more than three to four units a day and women no more than two to three units a day. It is also suggested that having one or two alcohol free days per week is wise.

The unit of alcohol measure is used to determine medical guidelines as to what are supposed to be safe levels of drinking for men and women per week.

Six Elements of Brief Interventions

1 Feedback: on how their drinking affects his or her health or how they are perceived by others.

2 Responsibility: to advise the individual that their drinking is their own responsibility.

3 Advice: on how to reduce or stop using drugs inform of services or help.

4 Menu: of services, options, youth services.

5 Empathy: a warm reflective and understanding approach is likely to encourage someone to change.

6 Self-efficacy: encourage young person of realising their ability rather than focussing on their weaknesses.

Alcohol and the Law

* Young people drink mainly beer, cider, lager and wine.
* Young people are choosing stronger drinks such as white cider, strong brands of beer, fruit wines and vodka.
* Although young people may at times drink in an uncontrolled way, most will not go on to develop serious problems.
* Under the age of 14 children are not permitted into the bar area of a pub unless the pub has a children's certificate. In this case they can enter if they are accompanied by an adult.
* At 14 you can enter a bar or pub but only if the landlord agrees and if you drink soft drinks (this can include low-alcohol drinks).
* At 16 you can buy beer, cider, or perry (made from pears) in a restaurant or eating area of a pub where there is no bar, if you are ordering a main meal.
* At 18 you can legally buy drinks in a pub, bar or off licence. If you are having problems getting served in pubs and you are over 18 you could apply for a proof of age card from the Portman Group, an organisation set up by the drinks industry.

Uses and Abuses of Alcohol quiz

Grouping
Whole group and small groups of three

Materials
Score Board, Squeaky Toys, Quiz Sheet/Answers

Purpose of exercise
• To evaluate existing knowledge of participants
• To help increase the knowledge of the participants
• To encourage participants to engage in debate and share their different views

Activity
• Participants in small group to discuss questions and decide as a group on answers.
• The quiz takes the form of a quiz show, with a person asking the questions and another person scoring.
• The main group is then divided into smaller groups.
• Each group is given a squeaky toy as a buzzer.
• The person asking the questions then explains the rules.
• The questions are read out. The first group to squeak their toys gets the first opportunity to answer the question. If the answer is incorrect, its open to other groups.
• Discussion
The score is then tallied and the final score is given.

NB After each answer, the person asking the questions takes time to go into depth in explaining the answer.

Alcohol Quiz
Tick the correct answer:
1. **T/F** 920,000 children live in a home where one or more parents are drinkers.
2. **T/F** Alcohol is a depressant which slows down the body's system.

3. **T/F** Drinking coffee or taking a cold shower can help you sober up.

4. **T/F** The first non-distilled alcohol beverages were made inadvertently, due to natural fermentation.

5. **T/F** It takes four hours for one unit of alcohol to leave your body.

6. **T/F** In the 18th century, alcohol was seen as a good thing, but drunkenness and social disorder were not.

7. **T/F** Alcohol related illnesses and injuries cost the NHS up to £3bn a year on hospital services.

8. **T/F** Alcohol causes liver damage.

9. **T/F** The gin epidemic hit London's streets in the early 1900's.

10. **T/F** Alcohol has the same effect on both men and women.

Alcohol Quiz Answers

1. **TRUE** Source: The National Association for children of Alcoholics 2000

2. **TRUE** Alcohol is a depressant drug which affects judgement and coordination.

3. **FALSE** Alcohol has to leave the body naturally.

4. **TRUE** The first beers where produced in Egypt 5,000 to 6,000 years B.C.

5. **FALSE** It takes one hour for one unit of alcohol to leave the body.

6. **TRUE** With the coming of the industrial age, drinking was less tolerated because of work performance and safety.

7. **TRUE** Source: Royal College of Physicians

8. **TRUE** The liver becomes enlarged and tender leading to possible liver failure.

9. **FALSE** The gin epidemic was in the 1700's.

10.**FALSE** Women are affected quicker as they have less fluid in their bodies so the alcohol absorbs faster.

Alcohol-Related Influences on Young People

Grouping
Large group to brief trainees and small groups of four for exercises.

Materials
Sugar paper, pens, empty alcohol bottles and cans, old magazines, newspapers.

Method
• Group discussion, presentations, small group work.
• To make use of the various experiences of group members in the learning process

Purpose of exercise
To consider reasons why people may choose to drink or not to drink alcohol

Activity 1
• Give each of the groups a topic to discuss and brainstorm. Five minutes for each group.
• Group 1 – why young people may choose to drink
• Group 2 – why young people may choose not to drink alcohol
• Group 3 – how young people could be influenced by family or culture to drink or not to drink
• Group 4 – how young people are influenced through media and advertising to drink alcohol.

Activity 2
• Ask each group to create an anti-drink campaign using bottles, cans, newspapers; they can role-play an advert, create a poster, or do an improvisation for other young people or adults.

Activity 3
• Ask group members to do a five minute presentation or sketch to the whole group about their campaign.

Example Prompt cards for activity one

Group 1
Why young people may choose to drink alcohol.
- Curiosity
- Peer pressure
- Have fun
- Get drunk
- Courage
- Boredom
- Take risks

Group 2
Why young people may choose to drink alcohol.
- Curiosity
- Peer pressure
- Have fun
- Get drunk
- Courage
- Boredom
- Take risks

Group 3
How young people could be influenced by family or culture to drink or not to drink
- Culture drinking down the pub every week
- Religious beliefs no influences
- Older brother/sister introduction to drinking
- Family member has serious problem

Group 4
How young people are influenced through media and advertising to drink alcohol.
- Television soap operas in pubs
- Adverts on TV
- Magazines making alcohol look attractive
- Packaging and flavouring
- Availability and cost

Strengths Units of Alcohol

Grouping
Large group

Materials
Play your drinks right cards, score sheet, flip chart pens

Method
Harm reduction exercise, large group game. Explain to young people that in reality they may choose to start drinking both recreationally or socially.

Purpose of exercise
In order to promote harm reduction, it's always useful to provide information in a useful non-threatening way.

Activity
Write on chart and explain to young people that all alcoholic drinks contain pure alcohol (ethanol) and alcohol by volume. One way of comparing the amount of alcohol in different types of drink is by using 'Units'.

- A small glass of wine (9% ABV) = 1 Unit.
- A 25ml pub measure of spirit(40% ABV) = 1 Unit.
- A half pint of ordinary strength lager/beer/cider (3.5% ABV) = 1 Unit.

Split the group in half and give each group half the 'play your drinks right' cards.

- Ask the groups to arrange themselves in a line in order of strength of units per drink.
- Use score sheet to provide correct answers. Discussion
- Ask the group to think about the recommended daily benchmarks for adults.
- Write up three to four units for men, two to three for women.
- Explain binge drinking is when on one occasion men or women drink 6-8 units at a time.
- For under 18's, binge drinking often means drinking to intoxication.

Alcohol Strengths and Units Score Card

Alcoholic Drink	Units	ABV % vol	Size
Sherry	0.9	Alc17.5%	50ml glass
Red wine	1.5	Alc12%	50ml glass
White wine	1.5	Alc12%	125ml glass
Tennents	4.0	Alc 9%	440ml can
Champagne	1.5	Alc 12%	125ml glass
Heineken	2.0	Alc 3.5%	1 pint 568ml
Strong K Cider	1.8	Alc 8.5%	275ml bottle
Bacardi Breezer	1.7	Alc 5%	330ml standard bottle
Rum	0.9	Alc 37.5%	25ml glass
Vodka	0.9	Alc 37.5%	25ml glass
Brandy	1.0	Alc 40%	25ml glass
Budweiser	1.5	Alc 5%	(275ml)bottle
Gin	0.9	Alc 37.5%	25ml glass
Stella Artois	1.5	Alc 5%	330ml standard bottle

Alcohol Law
Grouping
Large group, two teams.

Materials
'Play your drinks right' cards and 'question' and 'answer' sheets.

Method
The 'play your cards right' game show and group discussion.

Purpose of exercise
In order to promote harm reduction, it's always useful to provide information in a useful non-threatening way.

Activity

• Allocate group roles: two teams, one host, and score keeper. All roles can be changed around as required.

• Explain the game: The host will ask a question and the first team to shout the answer will get to have a go at the 'higher' or 'lower' guesses.

• The opposing team members will each have one 'play your drinks right' card. The first one will be turned over, and the winning team will have to guess if the next card is either 'higher' or 'lower' in its alcohol strength.

• Once this has been completed, the host goes on to ask the next question, and continues in the same format until all questions have been asked.

Discussion

• As a whole group, invite the young people to share their thoughts about the quiz show and the issues and facts raised.

• As group participants if they could change the law, would they, how and why?

Warning Jokes

WARNING: The consumption of alcohol may make you think you are whispering when you are not.

WARNING: The consumption of alcohol may cause you to think you can sing.

WARNING: The consumption of alcohol may make you think you can logically converse with members of the opposite sex without spitting.

WARNING: The consumption of alcohol may create the illusion that you are tougher, smarter, faster, and better looking than everyone else.

Play Your Cards Right Question Sheet

1. Only under medical supervision can a under five year old be given alcohol.
True: it's illegal except under medical supervision.

2. Alcohol is a class C drug under the misuse of drugs act.
False: Alcohol is not identified as a classified drug.

3. There may be differences in alcohol effects depending upon where one drinks.
True : e.g. local bar, with family, hostile environment.

4. White pupils are the most likely of all ethnic groups in the UK to drink alcohol.
True: 'Youth Justice Board 2001'.

5. It costs British industry more than £2bn a year due to alcohol related absenteeism and poor work performance.
True: (A Maynard 1992).

6. At age 14 or 15 young people can go anywhere in a pub but not drink.
True .

7. You can buy beer or cider at 15 if eating a meal in a restaurant.
False: At 16 or 17 young people can buy beer or cider to drink with a meal in a restaurant, but not in a bar. In Scotland it applies to wine too.

8. At 17 you can buy alcohol in a supermarket.
False: It's against the law for anyone under 18 to buy or be sold alcohol in a pub, off licence, supermarket or other outlet.

9. Police officers are allowed to confiscate alcohol from anyone under 18 drinking in a public place.
True.

Play Your Drinks Right Cards:

Sherry	Red Wine	White Wine
Tennents	Champagne	Heineken
Strong K Cider	Bacardi Breezer	Rum
Vodka	Brandy	Budweiser
Gin	Stella Artois	

Chapter 5 – Neuro Linguistic Programming
What is NLP?

'Neuro' refers to the mind and how we organise our mental life. 'Linguistic' is about language, how we use it and how it affects us. 'Programming' is about our sequences of repetitive behaviour and how we act with purpose. So NLP is about connection, for our thoughts, speech and actions are what connect us to others, the world and the spiritual dimension.

The starting point of NLP is curiosity and fascination about people. It is the study of the structure of subjective experience. How do we do what we do? How do we think? How do we learn? How do we get angry? And how do outstanding people in any field get their results? To answer these questions NLP explores how we think and feel and studies or 'models' excellence in all walks of life. The answers can benefit our interventions with the young people we work with.

Origins of NLP

NLP began in the early 1970's when Richard Bandler, a student of psychology at the University of California, Santa Cruz, began working with John Grinder, then Assistant Professor of Linguistics. They developed a process, called 'modelling', by which they could discern the sequence of ideas and behaviour that enables a person to accomplish a particular task. Together they modelled three people: Fritz Perls, the innovative psychologist and originator of Gestalt therapy; Virginia Satir, the prime force behind family therapy; and Milton Erickson, a clinical hypnotherapist, whose ideas are continued in Ericksonian hypnotherapy. They also drew on the insights and ideas of many others, particularly Gregory Bateson, the British writer and thinker on anthropology, cybernetics and communications theory. Their first models dealt with verbal and non-verbal communication skills. Consequently, NLP has given rise to a trail of techniques that can be used both personally and professionally. They are used internationally in fields such as sports, business, sales, and education, and enable us not only to reach out and influence others, but also to reach in and unify all the different parts of ourselves.

The Physiology of Thinking

How we think shows in our physiology. Here is the NLP presupposition:

The mind and body are one system

Visual Thinking

People who are visualising will tend to be looking up or at level and their neck muscles are likely to be contracted. They may also furrow their brow as if trying to focus on something. People who spend a lot of time visualising may complain of headaches or stiff neck. Breathing is a critical part of physiology. When visualising, people tend to stand or sit erect and breathe high in the chest. Breathing like this results in shorter, more shallow breaths, so people who are visualising will tend to breathe and speak more quickly.

Auditory Thinking

Auditory thinkers tend to make small rhythmic movements of the body, often swaying from side to side. The voice tonality will be clear, expressive, and often musical. Do you know anyone who habitually puts their head on one side when they think? Some people will lean their head on their hands as if on the telephone. They are listening to voice and sounds inside their head. You may also see their lips move as they form the words they are saying to themselves.

Kinesthetic Thinking

Kinesthetic thinking is thinking with the body and will usually involve a rounded, even slumped posture. When people think this way, they will often look downwards, for this helps to get in touch with bodily feelings. They will tend to breathe abdominally, low in the body, and the voice if often lower and slower, because abdominal breathing is fuller and slower.

I do not suggest that there is such a thing as universal body language. We all use these 'representational' systems and very many people will habitually favour one system. This being so, their physiology may take on some of these characteristics.

Representation System Physiology

	Visual	Auditory	Kinesthetic
Posture	Head up erect	Often swaying, rounded head to one side (telephone position)	Head down
Breathing	High in chest	Mid range	Low in abdomen
Voice and Tonality	Fast voice, higher pitched	Melodic rhythmic	Lower and softer
Eye movements	Up or defocus	Midline or down left	Down or down right

Eye Accessing Cues

NLP suggests that there is a link between the way our eyes move and the way we think. Eye movements are known as eye accessing cues in NLP, because they enable us to access certain information. They cue us.

(This is as you look directly at another person)
Visual eye accessing cues:

Auditory eye accessing cues:

Kinesthetic eye accessing cues:

Internal Dialogue eye accessing cues:

Particular eye movements are linked to particular representational systems. In general, people will look upwards or defocus when they visualise. They will move their eyes sideways or to the left or right when hearing sounds internally and they may look down to their right when thinking kinesthetically. Looking down to their left usually signifies internal dialogue. These movements are consistent and mostly unconscious. They are the general patterns, so do not take these as true for everyone.

What are the practical applications of eye accessing cues? You can use them not only to find out how others are thinking but also to make it easier for yourself to think in particular ways; you are literally tuning in your body and mind, like tuning into a television programme. When you need to visualise, look up. When you need to contact your feelings, look down. Use accessing cues to help you think more precisely and clearly in the way you want to.

Speaking Your Mind

Language is rich and flexible and there are many different ways to express our thoughts. People often express the same idea differently using language from different representational systems. For example, we have friends who say 'Be seeing you' (visual). Some say 'I'll be hearing from you' (auditory). Others say 'I'll be in touch' (Kinesthetic).

NLP understands language as a reflection of inner experience. It is a surprisingly accurate translation of the way we think.

The words and phrases that show which internal sense we are using are called predicates and predicate phrases in NLP. On page 95 is a table illustrating some common predicates to show you how they sound, so you can get a feel for the idea.

Logical levels

We build relationships on different levels. The American researcher and NLP trainer Robert Dilts uses a series of what he calls neurological levels that have been widely adopted in NLP thinking. They are very useful for thinking about building rapport and personal change.

The first level is the environment (the where and when)

The environment is the place we are in and the people we are with. You have probably heard people say that they were in the 'right place at the right time'. They are attributing their success to their environment at this level, shared circumstances build rapport.

The second level is behaviour (the what)

This is the level of our specific, conscious actions: what we do. In NLP behaviour includes thoughts as well as actions. What we do is not random; our behaviour is designed to achieve a purpose, although this may not always be clear, even to us. We may want to change our behaviour, smoking or constantly losing our temper, for example. But sometimes unwanted behaviour may be difficult to change because it is closely connected with other neurological levels.

The third level is capability (the how)

This is the level of skill: behaviour that we have practised so often it has become consistent, automatic and often habitual. This includes thinking strategies and physical skills. We all have many basic intrinsic skills, such as walking and talking, and also consciously learnt skills, such as reading or playing a musical instrument.

The fourth level is beliefs and values (the why)

This is the level of what we believe is true and what is important to us. Beliefs and values direct our lives to a considerable extent, acting both as permissions and prohibitions. Are there some skills you would like to develop, but think you can't?

The fifth level is identity (the who)

Have you heard someone say something like 'I am just not that kind of person'? That is an identity statement. Identity is your sense of yourself, your core beliefs and values that define who you are and your mission in life. Your identity is very resilient, although you can build, develop and change it.

Finally, the sixth level is the spiritual level

This is your connection to others and to that which is more than your identity, however you choose to think of it. Rapport at this level is described in spiritual literature as being one with humankind, the universe or God.

Changing levels

Knowing the logical levels is very useful in personal change and personal development work. Change is possible at any level. The question is, which will have the most leverage, that is, give the greatest result for the smallest effort? A change at the belief level is likely to affect skills and behaviour a great deal, a change in identity even more so. You can work from the top down or from the bottom up; all the levels relate together systemically.

Visual words and phrases	look focus dim see watch colour imagination	notice illustrate reveal perspective blank insight	• I see what you mean. • Something to look forward to. • The future looks bright.
Auditory Words and phrases	deaf loud speechless remark discuss	say silence listen music harmony	• On the same wavelength. • Turn a deaf ear. • Speak your mind. • Word for word. • Loud and clear. • What do you say?
Kinesthetic words and phrases	touch solid warm cold rough grasp hold	heavy weak hot smooth move gentle	• Get to grips with the idea. • Hold on a moment. • A cool customer. • Put your finger on it. • Heated argument. • A smooth operator.
Olfactory words and phrases	nose smell pungent fragrant		• Smell a rat. • Smelling of roses. • Nose for business.
Gustatory words and phrases	spicy sweet bitter salty		• A bitter experience. • A taste of the good life.

Rapport

NLP uses the word rapport, as we have seen, to describe a relationship of trust and responsiveness. Rapport is essentially meeting individuals in their model of the world. We all have different upbringings, experiences and ways of being. We are all unique, with different beliefs, capabilities and identities. We all see the world differently. To gain rapport with others you need to acknowledge them and their view of the world. You do not have to agree with it, just recognize and respect it. Rapport can be established (or broken) at many different levels.

Body language

We build rapport, and therefore trust, in a face-to-face meeting in many ways: with our words, our body language and our voice tone. The words are the most obvious part of any conversation, yet they are only the tip of the communication iceberg. One of the keys to good relationships is acknowledging others and giving them the attention they deserve. One way excellent communicators do this is by matching body language with the person they are with. Adopt a similar posture. Give the same amount of eye contact. Match the speed and general frequency of hand gestures. Matching is not mimicry, however. Exact copying is not respectful. People quickly notice it and think you are mocking them. Mismatching is the opposite of matching. It is also a useful skill. Do you want a way to extricate yourself from a conversation without appearing rude? Mismatch body language. Looking away or increasing the rate of head nodding are some ways.

Voice

We can also establish rapport with others by matching their voice tone. We do this to some extent without thinking. When your companion is soft spoken, it is natural to moderate your own voice. Voice matching is notmimicry, more like two instruments harmonizing. The easiest way to experiment is to match the volume and the speed of the other person's voice.

Words

Words can also establish rapport. First, using the same technical vocabulary, where appropriate, is one way of establishing professional credibility. Secondly, people will often mark out words and phrases that are important to them. Using the same words or phrases in your reply shows them you hear and respect their meaning.

Pacing and leading

Matching body language, voice tonality and words, and respecting beliefs and values are examples of what NLP calls pacing. Pacing is having the flexibility to meet others in their model of the world, rather than expecting them to fit in with yours. Pacing establishes a bridge. Once you have that, you can lead another person to other possibilities. You cannot lead without first pacing and gaining rapport.

Congruence

What would it mean to pace and lead yourself - to be in rapport with yourself? Rapport between mind and body is called congruence in NLP. Congruence means that your body language, tonality and words carry the same message. Your beliefs and values line up with your actions. However, congruence is not perfection. It is not that all of you is playing exactly the same tune, but all the parts of you are at least following the same score.

Multiple descriptions

Central to NLP is an appreciation of the value of having different points of view of the same event. This is called having a multiple description. NLP distinguishes three main points of view: to be able to act wisely you need all three perspectives.

* First position is your own reality. Think of a time when you were intensely aware of what you thought and believed, regardless of other people. You have just experienced being in first position, regardless of exactly what you thought about.
* Second position is taking another person's point of view. You think, 'How would this appear to them?' Matching body language helps in taking second position. Because communication is an

interactive process, the more you can understand how the other person is thinking and feeling, the better you can communicate to get what you both want from the interaction.

• Third position is the ability to take a detached point of view and appreciate the relationship between you and the other, and to have a different relationship with yourself. This is an important skill.

That is Not What I Meant At All...

Rapport is the first step in good communication. Have you been in a situation where you said something you thought was clear, only to be amazed at the response? An innocent remark is taken personally or a well meant offer of help refused with a reply like 'Don't interfere!' The offer was clear to you but not to the listener. This can happen in reverse as well, when what you understood was not what the other person meant.

When we communicate, our goal is to transmit meaning. How do we know we have succeeded? When the other person gets that message. A sender cannot decide what the signal will actually mean to the other person, only what they would like it to mean. There is no such thing as failure in communication – you always succeed in communicating something. It just may not be what you intended to put across. The responses you get give you valuable pointers about what to do next. They are your teachers. One NLP presupposition sums this up:

> **The meaning of the communication
> is the response you get.**

What would be the consequences of acting as if this NLP presupposition is true?

You might get curious. How are misunderstandings possible? And how can they be prevented? This is usually done by paying attention to the other person's response. You could pick up any misunderstandings before going miles out of your way and before they have serious consequences.

This is important in business, for example, where managers want to motivate rather than to antagonize their colleagues, and where miscommunication about prices and quantities of goods can result in large financial losses.

Exploring relationships

A relationship is two people eliciting responses from each other. If you want a change in response, then you must change your own actions. This will change the meaning for the other person and the spell is broken. Most of us have a relationship where we think, 'If only that person would stop acting that way, then everything would be fine.' It may be a family member or a work colleague. Think of a relationship like that to explore further.

What do you think it is about their behaviour that is the problem? For example, you may feel they are aggressive, insensitive or fault finding, so you may feel browbeaten, angry or irritated. Label both your own and the other person's behaviour. You might wonder at which logical level you are threatened. Is this an identity issue for you? Or does it challenge your beliefs and values? Even thinking about this relationship can put you into an unresourceful state. You do not want to carry that into what you do next, so think of something different. Move, shake off that feeling. In NLP this is called changing state.

Secondly, imagine what the relationship is like from the other person's point of view. This is going to the second position. How do they experience your behaviour? What sort of label would they put on it? How do they feel? Shake off that emotional state before continuing. Now, go outside the relationship, become a detached observer. This is going to the third position. A good way to do this is to imagine both of you on a stage. See how you respond to each other.

Shift your question from 'How can I change that person's behaviour?' to 'How am I reinforcing or triggering that person's behaviour?' How else could you respond? What prompts your behaviour?

When you communicate you are seeking to influence another person: you have an outcome in mind. Deciding what you want is the second pillar of NLP.

Getting in a State

A state is your way of being at any moment; the sum of your thoughts, feelings, emotions, mental and physical energy. States vary in intensity, length and familiarity. Some have names, for example, love, fascination, alertness, anger, jealousy, fatigue or excitement, while others are less easy to pin down – we may feel in a 'good mood' or a 'bad mood' or just 'out of sorts'. The state you are in is very important. It affects your health, the quality of your decisions and how successfully you carry out a task.

Everyone knows we respond to outside events, becoming angry, excited, loving or exasperated in response to other people and situations. But not so many realize that we can change our state at will. This has far-reaching implications for how we affect others and how successful we are in the world.

The next two NLP principles go together:

> **Having choice is better than not having choice.**
> **People make the best choice they can at the time.**

When you have choice about your state, you have more emotional freedom. The choices people make are limited by the states they find themselves in. When we increase the range of choice - and so increase our emotional freedom - we will have more, perhaps better, choices.

Becoming Aware

If you want to change your present state, the first thing is to become aware of it, for you cannot deliberately change a state you are unaware of.

Start from where you are. Explore the state you are in at the moment. Give it a name. Be aware of your body. Notice the feelings you have in the different parts of your body. If you are uncomfortable, change position. Now be aware of any mental pictures you might have. Do not try to change them. Become aware of any internal voices or sounds. How much mental and physical space do you have? Get a sense of your boundaries.

Now you have turned the spotlight of consciousness on your state, notice how it has changed.

Your Baseline State

Some states you 'visit' more than others and there are a small number that you return to regularly. Of these, one will be your baseline state, that familiar state where you feel most at home. Is your home a comfortable and wellfurnished one? If it had a name, what would it be? Is your baseline state balanced and harmonious or do you habitually feel unbalanced and incongruent? What do you like about it and what would you add if you could?

When your baseline state is long established, it can seem the only way to be, instead of only one way to be. If you are uncomfortable in your baseline state, remember you can change it like any other and custom design one that is a pleasure to return to.

Anchors

The two most important questions so far are, 'What state do I want to be in to make best use of what is happening to me?' and then, 'How can I arrange it?'

Our states are constantly changing as we react to the environment. To have choice about your state, you need to know what triggers it.

The sight and sound of certain things will change your state. NLP calls any stimulus that changes our state an anchor. An anchor may be visual, like the sight of a newborn baby or holiday photographs. It may be auditory, like an advertising jingle, or kinesthetic, like a handshake or a relaxing massage. It may be olfactory, like the smell of roses, or gustatory – a particular taste that evokes a specific feeling or memory. It may be external, in the environment, or internal, within the mind, and it can operate at every logical level - for example, your name is an anchor for your identity, and religious symbols are anchors for beliefs and values.

Some anchors are almost universal. What makes them universal is our human ability to link stimulus to response without thinking, so you do not have to evaluate every stimulus you receive. Do you evaluate a red traffic light every time you see one?

We consciously choose very few of our anchors, they have been built up randomly throughout our lives. Many of them are neutral and some trigger unresourceful states. Many anchors are linked to the past and may be out-ofdate.

The first practical step is to become aware of the anchors that put you in an unresourceful state. Once you know them, you can choose whether or not to respond. The second step is to design your own anchors.

Using Anchors to Change State

Using anchors is the key to designing, changing and choosing your baseline state, or any other state you wish. Choose the resources you want, associate them to an anchor, and then consistently use that anchor to bring those resources into the present moment. The NLP presupposition is:

> ## We either already have all the resources
> ## we need or we can create them.

What is difficult sometimes is bringing them to where they are needed. There are three ways to access resources.

Find a Role Model

You may have got your baseline state from a role model without realizing. Now you can pick one that appeals to you. It can be a real or fictional character. 'Try on' that character for size. What would it be like to be that character? What sort of state allows them to act as they do? What could you take that is valuable for you?

Use Your Physiology

This is the physical approach to states. Changing your physiology is the most direct way of changing your state. A stuck state, will show in stuck physiology; getting up and moving is the simplest action to change state. Smiling broadly, looking up and standing straight will change your state. Acting as if you feel good can start to produce those very feelings.

Change Your Thinking

One way to do this is to 'think of a time when...' For example, think of an experience you want to remember and enjoy. Go back into that scene, making sure you are 'associated' in the memory, i.e. seeing through your own eyes. Hear the sounds and voices and enjoy the good feelings again. On returning to the present you will have changed state.

Building a State with Anchors

Here is a process that will build a resource state. First you have to decide what state you want. What resources do you want? You might need to face a challenge with humour, patience or curiosity.

Remember a time when you had that state and get back to it – see what you saw, hear what you heard and get the feeling as strongly as you can. If necessary, think of a role model and imagine living an episode as them in the state you want. Now, change state by coming back to the present.

Decide what associations or anchors you want to trigger that state. Pick one thing you can see in your mind's eye (a visual anchor), one sound or word you can say to yourself (an auditory anchor) and one small inconspicuous gesture you can make (a kinesthetic anchor). Some people use a clenched fist or touch two fingers together.

Go back and fully experience that resourceful state. Just before the resourceful feeling reaches its peak, see the picture, hear the sound and make the gesture. Then change your physiology, change state and think of something else.

Test your anchors. See the picture, hear the sound and make the gesture and notice how this brings back the resourceful feeling. If you are not satisfied, do it again. Do this as many times as you need, until the anchors bring back the resourceful feeling.

You have now set up your own anchors so that whenever you see that picture, hear that sound and make that gesture, it puts you into the state you want. You do not need all three anchors; indeed, some people use only one anchor. Find out what works best for you.

Once you have the ability to choose and change your states, your life will be different. You will not be a victim, you will have moved the locus of control from outside to inside yourself.

Reality Leaves a Lot to the Imagination

Most human beings share the same five senses and the same basic neurology, yet see, hear and feel the world very differently. How do we make personal meaning from the events that befall us? First, we are not passive receivers of input, like a computer keyboard. We are active explorers of reality. Perception comes from the inside. Every single brain is unique, and as we search out what interests and is important to us, we strengthen certain neural connections in our brains and weaken others. We are drawn to those things that interest us.

Our senses are the channels through which we perceive the outside world. Aldous Huxley called them the 'doors of perception' – sight, hearing, feeling, taste and smell.

We process all information through our senses.

Our senses are receptive to certain aspects of whatever is out there. However, being conscious, we have the ability to decide which signals from the environment are the most important at a particular time and should come into our awareness over all the possible signals. We do not throw our doors of perception wide open because we would be totally overwhelmed. We have gatekeepers that we set on the doors: beliefs, values, interests, occupations and preoccupations all patrol the threshold to preserve us from sensory overload.

Our Map of Reality

What we finally perceive is a map of reality. Some parts are full of detail, others are sketchy and some may be completely empty. Having made our map, is it a good one? Is it well sign-posted and does it make it easy or difficult to get what we want? Reality Leaves a Lot to the Imagination. One of the most important NLP presuppositions is:

NLP is the art of changing our map for one that gives us more choice.

> **People respond to their map of reality and not to reality itself.**

Representational Systems

You make your map and you have to live in it. Remember two things as you create it:

1 How you use your senses on the outside is going to affect your thinking and experience on the inside.

2 You can change your experience by changing how you use your senses on the inside.

We have an incredible ability to create experience on the inside. A painful memory will make us wince again. A pleasant memory will make us smile and re-experience the pleasure. We represent our experience to ourselves using our senses, so in NLP the senses are called representational systems.

Know Yourself and Pace Others

Sensory-based language is a powerful tool in communicating and influencing. First, know yourself. Find out your own language and thinking preferences. You can do this by writing or speaking into a recorder for a few minutes about your personal and professional life. Don't think about it, just write or say whatever comes into your head. Then notice what language predominates – seeing, hearing or feeling.

Start to notice how others express their thoughts. A person will consistently use language from their preferred representational system, so listening to them is the easiest way to find out which one they favour. Listen past the content of what a person says to how they say it. Once you have developed an ear for sensory language you will be able to pace others with language. Use words from the same representation system as they do. This will give you rapport on the verbal level. For example, someone says, 'I can't tell if this is right for me.' You reply, 'What more do you need to hear?' If they were to talk instead about getting a clear vision and then moving forward, you would pace them by talking in terms of seeing the way forward. Thought connects with physiology and both connect with language.

Using Submodalities

Submodalities offer tremendous opportunities for gaining control of our subjective experience because we can change them at any time. Take, for example, your experience of a negative state, say, boredom. How is it possible to experience boredom?

An Exercise

Make yourself comfortable and remember a pleasant memory. Look at your mental picture of it. If you find it hard to visualize, see whatever you can. Is the picture black and white or is it in colour? Is it moving or still? How bright is it?

Are you looking at the scene through your own eyes or areyou seeing yourself in the picture? These are all examples of visual submodalities. Let the picture fade.

Now listen to any sounds and voices in your memory. Are they loud or soft, near or far? Are they continuous? Are they clear or muffled? From which direction do they come? These are auditory submodalities. Let the sounds fade.

Now the feelings. Whereabouts in your body are they located? Is each feeling large or small? Warm or cool? How intense is it? How large is the area it covers? These are kinesthetic submodalities. Let these feelings fade. What is left?

Our memories, hopes and beliefs all have a submodality structure, and this is how we give them meaning. Then we have feelings about them. This is true whether they are unique events, for example, 'my first date', or classes of experience, for example, 'love', 'beliefs', 'confusion' or 'hobbies'.

Some of the most common submodality distinctions are listed on the following pages. There may also be others that are important to you.

Whatever the outside cause, the state itself will have a submodality structure.

For example, when people describe being bored, they will typically talk about everything being 'flat' or 'grey'. They will use a typical tone of voice.

To change a state of boredom, determine its submodality structure in all representational systems. Then think of a state you would rather be in, for example, curiosity. Think of something you are very curious about and again determine the submodality structure of that state. Now take a step back and look at both sets of submodalities. How are they different? Go back to the bored experience (if you still can) and change the submodalities of boredom to those of curiosity. Notice how your experience is different.

When you are in a bored state, you cannot 'make' yourself curious by will-power, however much you may want to be. But changing submodalities gives you the practical means to change your state.

> **When we change the structure of the experience by changing the submodalities, then the meaning will also change. When the meaning changes, our internal response will also change.**

Associated and Dissociated States

Association and dissociation are two very important submodalities. You are associated when you are inside an experience, seeing through your own eyes. You are dissociated from an experience when you are outside it, seeing yourself at one remove.

An associated experience is very different from a dissociated experience. When you are associated, you are in the experience and you get the bodily feelings, good or bad, 'associated' with the experience. Store pleasant memories as associated pictures to enjoy them again.

When you are dissociated, you are outside the experience and do not experience the accompanying feelings. You might have wondered how it is possible for some people to look back on important and intense experiences and say they feel nothing. They do it by dissociating. Dissociating can be very useful; it keeps the feelings from painful memories at bay. It also enables you to learn from experience.

Modelling

In NLP, modelling means finding out how someone does something. It is the core of NLP, the process of replicating excellence. Modelling a skill means finding out how the person who has the skill thinks about it, and the beliefs and values that enable them to do it. You can also model emotions, experiences, behaviour, beliefs and values. NLP models what is possible. It is possible because human beings have already done it. The NLP presupposition is:

> **Modelling successful performance leads to excellence. If one person can do something it is possible to model it and teach it to others.**

To model a skill you focus on three neurological levels: what the model does (their behaviour and physiology), how they do it (the way they think) and why they do it (beliefs and values). You will also need to take into account the environment and the identity of the model.

To model a skill you need:
- the model's behaviour and physiology
- the way they think
- their beliefs and values

NLP modelling has three main phases. The first phase is observing, questioning and being with the model when they are actually engaged in the skill you are interested in. You take second position with the model, becoming them as far as you are able. Direct questioning on its own can be disappointing, for a person who is very skilful has usually forgotten the learning stages and is unaware of exactly how they do the task. The work of the NLP modeller is to go beyond this barrier of consciousness and learn about the unconscious competence of the model.

When you have finished the first phase you will have a lot of information, and you will not yet be sure what is important and what is not. Some elements may be the personal style of the model. So the second phase is systematically to take out each facet of the model's behaviour to find out whether it makes a difference to the results you get. if it does, then it is an essential part of the model. If it does not, then it can be relinquished.

Mental Strategies

The third and final phase is to analyse what you have learned so that you can teach it to others.

There is an alternative way of modelling, which works better for some skills. Here you break down the task into small pieces and systematically set about acquiring them one by one until you have built the whole skill. Once you have the skills of modelling, you can use them to model whatever interests you.

Finding out how a person thinks - their mental strategies – is an important part of modelling. Mental strategies are how you organize your thoughts and actions to accomplish a task – from something simple, such as remembering a name, to something very complex, such as planning a career or falling in love. Just as large goals decompose into smaller tasks, complex strategies contain a number of smaller ones, like a series of Chinese boxes one inside another.

To model a strategy you need to discover:
- the representation systems used
- the submodalities of the inner pictures, sounds and feelings
- the sequence of steps

Motivation Strategies

Have you ever wondered how you motivate yourself to do something? Your motivation strategy will determine how easily you can get down and do a task. For example, one person we modelled looks first at the work she needs to do and hears a loud, encouraging, internal voice saying, 'Time to do this.' Then she constructs a big, bright, shiny mental picture of the finished work. Feeling good as she looks at that picture, she starts the work. This strategy works well and it pleasant to run. It moves towards a positive purpose. This brings us to another NLP presupposition:

> **People work perfectly. No one is wrong or broken. It is a matter or finding out how they function so that this can effectively be changed to something giving more useful or desirable results.**

The Gatekeepers at the Doors of Perception

How do we create our model of the world from our experience? NLP suggests there are three gatekeepers at the doors of perception.

The first is Deletion

We are selective about our experience and leave parts out – we delete them. Either they do not register or we discount them as unimportant.

The second is Distortion

We change our experience, amplifying or diminishing it, and seeing it differently, as if in a fairground hall of mirrors.

The third is Generalization

We take certain aspects of our experience as representative of a whole class and pay no attention to exceptions. This is useful because it lets us respond to new situations on the basis of what we have learned from similar ones in the past. It is a problem if we generalize wrongly or do not stay open to new experience. Beliefs are examples of generalizations, These gatekeepers are neither good nor bad in themselves; they are both an asset and a liability.

If we did not delete some sensory information we would be overwhelmed. However, we may be deleting just what we need to pay attention to, for example, how we are feeling or important feedback from others.

In the same way, if we did not distort we would stifle our creativity. When you are planning to redecorate, it is useful to have an idea of what a room is going to look like when it is finished. This is sensory distortion. But if you decide that when someone looks at you in a certain way they are really despising you, you run the risk of distorting the meaning of their look and then distorting your response.

When you generalize you aim to make sense of the world and know what to expect. This means that when you encounter a door handle that is differently shaped from any you have seen before, you do not have to retire puzzled. You know that it is just another kind of handle.

So generalization is a basic part of how we learn. But the same process can spell disaster. Suppose you had a difficult relationship and decided on the basis of that experience that all men or all women are the same – not to be trusted. Your generalization could stop you seeking out men and women who are exceptions to your rule. So, through deleting, distorting and generalizing we can create a friendly or a hostile world. And the more we practise, the better we will get at making the world fit our filters.

People have biases on how they shape their perceptions. Some people will do more deleting, while others tend to distort more and yet others will be more given to generalization.

Language

NLP suggests these three gatekeepers transform sensory experience into internal representations. They also transform our internal representations when we use language. First we delete, distort and generalize our experience. Then our choice of words to describe the experience deletes, distorts and generalizes it all over again. Spoken language, then, is a map of a map and two levels away from sensory experience.

The world does not come with labels attached. We attach them and then forget we did so. We can mistake the words we attach to our experience for the experience itself and allow them to direct our actions.

We can use language in three ways to find out about and influence experience. Firstly, we can ask questions that connect language with thought and back to sensory experience. For example, someone says to you, 'The people here are unfriendly.' This is a generalization, and we can ask a specific question like, 'Do you mean everybody? Is there no one at all here who is friendly?' This will make the person look at their generalization and see what basis it has in their experience. They will have to look at specific instances. This is called chunking down in NLP, going from a general case to more specific ones.

The second way we can use language is to go from specific instances to more general ones. We can use very permissive and vague language that allows the other person to find just that particular meaning that is right for them. This is called chunking up, going from a particular case to a general one.

Finally we can use language to chunk sideways: to compare one experience with another. This is the realm of metaphor, simile and storytelling, where you explain, allude or illuminate by comparison.

Language, Trance and Stories

As we have seen, language is very powerful, you cannot not respond to it. When we hear something we have to make some meaning out of it, so we search unconsciously for the way it could be relevant to us. The vaguer it is, the more possible meanings it has.

The Milton Model

NLP has studied this vague type of language and produced the Milton Model. The Milton Model is a way of constructing sentences that are rife with deletions, distortions and generalizations. It originated from the modelling work done by Richard Bandler and John Grinder on Milton Erickson's artfully vague use of language.

Milton Erickson was one of the foremost hypnotherapists of the last century. A client goes to a therapist because they cannot solve their problem consciously on their own. The resources they need are unconscious. Erickson used language to pace and lead the person's reality. He described their ongoing sensory experience in very general terms and then led them deeper into their own internal reality. He used complex language to distract their conscious mind and allow access to the unconscious resources. When the client was in a trance, Erickson enabled them to search for the resources they needed from their unconscious with vague, open, permissive language and metaphors.

Trance

So the Milton Model originated in hypnotherapy and was used to induce trance. Trance is not a special state evoked only by skilled hypnotists after much concentration. It is a naturally occurring state that we slip into and out of all the time. When we are in a trance our attention is tightly focused on our internal world and any language pattern that increases our involvement with our own internal reality will deepen the trance.

Trance plays a big part in everyday life. For example, when you are watching television you are in a sort of trance, your attention is fixed on one point and you are 'gone' from the rest of the world. People may call your name and get no response, even though your ears are working normally. On other occasions there is some external distraction and you 'snap out' of your reverie.

The traditional signs of trance to look for are: body immobility, relaxed face, slowing reflexes, time distortion, feeling distanced or dissociated. However, it need not be exactly so, for example, a computer game is a very effective trance inducer.

Day-dreaming is a form of trance, usually a very creative one. When you day-dream, you are open to ideas from your unconscious. Many scientific breakthroughs happen this way – inventors report the solution that came to them in a flash as they were deeply immersed in the problem.

Everyday Trances

Rather than give a more detailed description of the Milton Model, we would like to look at trance in everyday life and the practical applications that follow. Some everyday trances we have control over - we can 'snap out' of them. Others catch and hold us. Some are productive and creative – and others are negative and unresourceful.

What are your everyday trances? Are there any unresourceful trances you repeatedly find yourself in?

Find out what triggers them. It could be external, for example, a particular critical tone of voice. It could be internal, a particular thought or memory. Trance triggers are like trapdoors – once you have fallen through, it is very difficult to get back. Catch the trance before it develops and do not associate into it. If you find you are in it, then acknowledge that and come out by focusing on the external world. When you are in the present moment, you are not in a trance. Remember the trance is not you. It is something you go into and so it is something you can come out of.

All our trances have some purpose, they are attempts to solve problems. Think about what the trance does for you. Respect the intention and change the behaviour.

Metaphor

Metaphor is used in NLP to cover figures of speech, stories, comparisons, similes and parables. Metaphors chunk sideways from one thing to another, making comparisons and connections that may be subtle or obvious. To make sense of our experience we need to make comparisons.

Stories are our birthright and metaphors pervade our thinking. They are woven into our lives at every level, from bedtime stories we listened to as children to the ways we think about work, life, relationships and health. They build creative connections between two events or experiences, giving another different, hopefully illuminating example. Take an example: Life is like ... How would you complete this and what would that mean? Is life like a bowl of cherries? A struggle? An adventure? A school? A test? A wheel? A jungle?

The metaphors a person uses give the key to their life and the way they think. A person to whom life is an adventure is going to approach events quite differently from a person for whom life is a struggle. Metaphors are not right or wrong, but they have consequences for how people think and act, consequences which are implicit in the metaphor.

Problem-solving

Think of a current difficult situation in your life. Think of your problem as a short metaphor. Quickly. Your problem is like ... A jam doughnut? A ringing telephone? A poker game? A fight with a dragon?

This is your present state. Now look at your metaphor. What are your assumptions inherent in that metaphor? What else would have to be true for that metaphor to be accurate?

Now think of what you would prefer the problem to be like. Quickly make another metaphor. You would prefer ... Now think how the problem is like that.

What are the differences between the first metaphor and the second metaphor? How could you get from one to the other? How are they similar? The connection could be the resource that helps you from one to the other.

Giving people instructions about what they 'should' do does not work. They know already, but it is just conscious mind information. A metaphor goes beyond conscious understanding.

For example, Ian was working with a married couple who were experiencing some difficulties in their relationship. Although they basically wanted to stay together, they found it difficult to cooperate. Ian tasked them to take dancing lessons together. Both had learned to dance a little in the past, but not with each other. Dancing was a metaphor for their relationship. As they learned to dance together, they physically learned the give and take, ebb and flow, lead and follow that they had lacked in their relationship.

Beliefs and Beyond

Beliefs have us. They drive our behaviour. They are intangible and frequently unconscious. They are often confused with facts. But while a fact is what happened, a belief is a generalization about what will happen. It is a guiding principle.

We share certain beliefs about the physical world based on facts. For example, fire burns and we are subject to the laws of gravity, so we do not tempt fate by walking off cliffs or putting our hands into a fire. However, we have many beliefs about ourselves and other people that control our behaviour just as effectively as the belief that fire burns, and these may or may not be true. It is these beliefs that NLP is interested in.

When people tell you they believe something, they are either telling you of a value they hold dear or their best guess in the absence of knowledge. Beliefs answer the question 'Why?'

Belief Formation
Beliefs are formed haphazardly throughout life from the meaning we give to our experience. They are formed during our upbringing from modelling significant others, especially our parents. They can be formed from a sudden unexpected conflict, trauma or confusion, and the younger we are, the more likely this is to happen. Sometimes beliefs are formed by repetition - the experience has no emotional intensity, but it just keeps happening, like water dripping on a stone.

Empowering and Limiting Beliefs
Some of our beliefs give us freedom, choice and open

possibilities. Others may be oppressive, closing down choice. Acting as if they were true makes you and others miserable. Beliefs are often expressed in the form: 'I can...', 'I can't...', 'I shouldn't...', 'I must...'

Take a moment to write down some examples you have of each of those four.

Do you get the sense that those that start 'I can't...' and 'I shouldn't...' limit your choices? Examine those beliefs. Ask yourself, 'What prevents me?' and 'What would happen if I did?' Even beliefs that begin 'I must...' may be problematic if you feel that this is so under all circumstances.

Belief Change

Would you like to change some of your beliefs for more liberating ones that make life a pleasure? The ability to choose and change your beliefs is one of the key tools NLP has to offer.

When you change a belief we suggest you replace it with another belief that keeps the positive intention of the old one. The new one must also be congruent with your sense of self.
To change a negative belief you need to ask yourself,'What is this belief doing for me?' and 'What belief would I rather have?' There are some good questions you can ask yourself before you consider changing any belief you have:

- 'How will my life be better with the new belief?'
- 'How might my life be worse with the new belief?'
- 'What is the best that could happen if I kept the old belief?
- 'What is the best thing that could happen with the new belief?'

NLP has a number of techniques for changing limiting beliefs. Some work by changing the submodality structures of the old and new beliefs. Another involves going back to the imprint experience that generated the belief and re-evaluating it from a resourceful position. Whatever the technique, it is important that the new belief fits with the person's values and sense of self.

Belief and Action

As already mentioned, beliefs drive behaviour. Sometimes we hold conflicting beliefs and then we will be incongruent. Sometimes people profess to believe in a particular value, but their behaviour contradicts it. Behaviour is belief in action, whatever we may consciously say we believe.

We generalize most of our beliefs, making them true or false in all contexts. Need this be so? As we have already mentioned, in NLP you can choose your beliefs. They are maps of reality. When we believe something we act as if it were true, but that does not make it true. Nor does it make it false. It will be true for you in that moment.

To understand the effect of beliefs, choose the ones you want carefully. Choose those that give you the life you wish for.

The final principle of NLP we want to address is one that makes all the others real:

> **If you want to understand - act.**

Because the learning is in the doing. Principles make a difference in action. For example, we hold core beliefs about our identity that have profound effects. 'I am basically a good person who makes mistakes sometimes' and 'I am a stupid person who sometimes gets it right by luck' will give very different experiences.

We also have beliefs about what lies beyond our identity. When Albert Einstein was asked what was the most important question for mankind to ask, he replied, 'The most important question facing humanity is: Is the Universe a friendly place?'

How we answer that question brings us to what it means to be a person and that takes us into the spiritual realm.

NLP and Spirituality
Throughout history people have searched, driven by the feeling that there is more to life than body and mind. We are constantly reaching out beyond ourselves to know by experience our connection and unity with that which is more than ourselves. What can NLP contribute?

NLP deals with the structure of human experience and so these major issues are very relevant. Were NLP to be silent about spiritual experience, it could give the message that spiritual experience is somehow different and removed from life. This is not so. NLP itself makes no claim on reality, truth, morality or ethics. It treats them as subjective experiences. It does not acknowledge or deny an external reality, but simply suggests you act as if the presuppositions are true and notice the results you get. NLP asks not 'Is it true?' but 'Is it useful?'

How you decide what you want and how you will achieve it are ethical and moral questions. How can we use NLP in the service of ethics and aesthetics? These are necessarily the responsibility of the NLP practitioner: we each apply our own morality and ethics to both our outcomes and the means we choose to achieve them. The basis for ethics is our common humanity and deepest essence as human beings.

Spirituality could be said to be about finding our basic humanity – the essence we share with every person. One way of thinking of it is as a feeling of being most truly ourselves and in the process discovering and becoming most deeply connected with others in their full magnificence. There are moments like this in most people's lives. You do not have to spend a lifetime of prayer and self-denial to have them. Some religious traditions hold that spiritual experiences are hard to come by, but they are all around – those splashes of joy and insight, those peak experiences when you feel most fully alive. Giving birth and becoming a parent, feeling your connection with life, looking into the eyes of a newborn child, these can all be spiritual experiences.

A universal metaphor for spiritual experience is a search, quest or journey and the end of our search, in the words of T. S. Eliot in 'The Four Quartets' will be to 'arrive where we started and know the place for the first time'. The answers on the outside are mirrored within us. Or, as Gertrude Stein put it, 'There never has been an answer, there never will be an answer – that's the answer.'

Promoting Achievement, Encouraging Success

For more information about the work of the Learning in Action Foundation, or to make a charitable donation, please contact us on 01483 723488. The Learning in Action Foundation is a registered charity number 1108531. Office address: 8 Darvel Close, Woking, Surrey GU21 4XG

Step up and be counted: young person confronting their issues and making steps towards lasting change

Award for outstanding achievement

Young Person encouraged voice the things hindering him from moving his life forward

Bibliography

Chapter 1

Aggleton, Hurry and Warwick (Eds.) (2000) *Young People and Mental Health*, Wiley

Casdagli, P and Gobey, F Grief, *Bereavement and Change: A quick Guide*, Daniels Publishing, 38 Cambridge Place, Cambridge CB2 1NS.

Geldard and Geldard (1997) *Counselling Adolescents*, Sage Publications.

Hawton, Keith (1986) *Suicide and Attempted Suicide Among Children and Adolescents,* Sage Publications.

Keir, N (1986) *I Can't Face Tomorrow: Help For Those With Thoughts Of Suicide And Those Who Counsel Them*, Thorsons Publishing Group.

Chapter 2

Berg, Insoo Kim (1994) *Family Based Services: A Solution focused approach. New York*, Norton.

Stuart, Dr E. (1992) *Daring to Speak Loves Name*, New York, Penguin

Iveson, Chris (1990) *Whose Life? Working with People,* London, BT Press

Chapter 3

Bono, C. (1998) *Family Outing. London*, Pan Books

Queen, C. and Schimel, L (1997) *Promosexuals*, San Francisco, Cleis Press

Stuart, Dr E. (1992) *Daring to Speak Loves Name*, New York, Penguin

Chapter 4

Aggleton, Hurry and Warwick (Eds) (2000) *Young People and Mental Health,* John Wiley & Sons.

Covey, Stephen R (2003) *Life Matters New York*, McGraw-Hill.

Iveson, Chris (1990) *Whose Life? Working with People.* London, BT Press.

Robbins, A (2001) *Get The Edge*, Guthy-Renker Corporation.